FOOTBALL AND CHESS
TACTICS; STRATEGY; BEAUTY

Adam Wells

HARDINGE SIMPOLE

Hardinge Simpole Publishing,
Aylesbeare Common Business Park,
Exmouth Road,
Aylesbeare,
Devon,
EX5 2DG,
England

admin@hardingesimpole.co.uk
http://www.hardingesimpole.co.uk

First published in December 2007
Reprinted with corrections April 2008.

ISBN-10   1 84382 186 9
ISBN-13 978 1 84382 186 1

For my father

ACKNOWLEDGEMENTS

I would like to thank
Miranda El-Rayess for her invaluable help;
Derek Copsey for his work and advice on the graphics;
Craig Smith for his enthusiasm and encouragement;
Professor Barbara Hardy for offering ideas and a
    far-reaching knowledge;
Ilan Shaki for happily discussing football tactics
    with me to an obsessive degree;
my sister for her sound advice,
and my brother for many good games
    of chess and football.

CONTENTS

INTRODUCTION

'I've got extra numbers in the middle ... I'm controlling that area ... but the defence is very well organised and it's hard to find any gaps ... I can't commit too much to attack though, because there is a strong chance of a quick counter-attack ... better to be patient and wait for an opening - surely they will make a mistake at some point ... maybe it would be good to use the flanks more, and try to stretch the defence that way ... the left side could be a bit suspect ... it should be exploited ... maybe there needs to be an increase in tempo and a bit more pressure applied ... the defence could be broken with a good combination at the right time ... perhaps one of the defenders could be dragged out of position ...'

This is an internal monologue. But who is this person and what is he doing? Football fans would have no hesitation in answering that it is a coach watching his team play and trying to work out a strategy for breaking down the opposition. After all, these are the kind of tactical ideas that we hear expressed regularly by football pundits, players and fans the world over. There is, however, another group of people who would have a completely different yet equally emphatic interpretation: these are clearly the thoughts of a person playing a game of chess. The truth is that both interpretations would be correct.

Upon closer inspection, similarities also appear between the more specific tactical elements of the games. 'If I can get my Knight onto f6 it will be in a major danger area, and other pieces will be able to build off it', a chess player might say to himself. Somewhere not too far away, a football coach simultaneously gives instructions to his attacking midfielder: 'you've got to get into the danger area just in front of the box. That way the strikers will be able to build off you more easily'. 'They're giving you space to come forward, so use it', another coach tells his central defender. Meanwhile a chess player considers whether to move his defensive pawn forward. 'It's protecting the King... but there is so much space in front of it... so maybe I should bring it out and let it contribute to the attack.'

In accordance with these similarities, there is a large overlap in the very specific terminology that analysts use to dissect the games. Television pundits such as Mark Lawrensen and David Pleat regularly use terms such as 'overloading', 'initiative', 'holes', 'controlling the game', 'combinations' and 'tempo'. These are all standard terms used in chess analysis. And where the terminology is not identical, often the concepts are nevertheless extremely similar.

Despite these similarities, many fans of one game have absolutely no interest in the other. Indeed, people tend to see the games as diametrically opposed. Numerous football fans see chess as slow, boring and devoid of energy. At the same time, chess enthusiasts often regard football as simple and mindless. This is not to say that the games have not been compared before. We often hear football commentators describe matches as 'chess-like'. However, these casual remarks certainly do not amount to a serious analysis and are often said in a derogatory manner.

For many football fans, Liverpool's comeback against AC Milan in the Champions League Final of 2005 contained all the elements of what people love so much about football: energy, courage, excitement, fighting spirit, unpredictability and the power of having a dream so strong that you can come back from 3-0 down against a superior team and win. Meanwhile, the antithesis of such a game would be what many commentators in modern football would describe as a tight, slow, 'chess-like' game in which teams create few scoring chances and the result is 0-0. However, to use chess as an analogy for unexciting football games is neither useful nor accurate. It clouds the fact that many exciting, high-scoring games also possess chess-like qualities. Liverpool's comeback against AC Milan, which I discuss later, was inspired primarily by principles that are inherently chess-like. The Liverpool manager Rafael Benitez did not bring about such a transformation in his team by making a rousing speech. He inspired it by analysing the game and changing it from a tactical point of view at half time. Everything that followed was a direct consequence of the chess-like repositioning of his players.

The relationship between chess and football is not an obscure idea that comes to mind whilst watching certain types of football. It is a permanently entrenched part of all football games, whether they are tight and slow or lively and open. By stripping the games down to their most basic structural components, we can find out just how real and extensive these similarities are. This may in turn offer us some explanation as to why the games are so aesthetically pleasing and meaningful to so many.

FOOTBALL AND CHESS

At the most fundamental level, football and chess are games that involve using **space** effectively and getting the **timing** right in order to break down an opponent's defence whilst preventing them from breaking down yours.

And that's it. There are very few limiting rules. There are no complicated scoring systems or procedures of play that have to be followed. It is clear-cut: you must capture pieces or score goals whilst staying within the confines of the board or pitch. How you choose to do this is entirely up to you. Since players have such freedom to do what they want, they are presented with a huge number of options of how to act in a given situation. Thus, it is the very simplicity of the games that paradoxically makes them so complex.

Aside from the freedom of choice that the games allow players, it is also the 'teamwork' element which creates their complexity. No other team sport places such an emphasis on harmony between players as football. As in chess, every movement or action affects everything else around it. One badly positioned piece or player can be ruinous. Consequently, a group of superior footballers will often lose to technically weaker players who are interacting more harmoniously. In the same way, as every serious chess player knows, having more powerful pieces left on the board does not guarantee a win. It is the power of the interactions between the pieces which is decisive. Perhaps it is no surprise that both Rafael Benitez and Karel Bruckner (longstanding coach of the Czech Republic national team) are both avid chess players, and know only too well how much greater the whole can be than the sum of the parts. Both are famous for their ability to create exceptional teams without exceptional players. Indeed, according to his agent, Benitez has no particular aptitude for noticing good players, such is his preoccupation with watching the team as a whole.

As a result of the endless possibilities of harmony and interaction, both games are limitless: infinitely complicated, infinitely interesting, forever elusive and mysterious, and always open to new interpretation. This makes them very exciting to play and watch.

And so, because in essence both games are based on the same concepts, if you are a fan of one game, it is likely that you will enjoy the other.

One of the popular misconceptions about chess is that it is a game of pure calculation. Either you have a brain that can work through ten moves ahead or you don't. This is not true. Of course, calculation is a large part of chess, but also important are positional knowledge, instinct and creativity. If two players with equal powers of calculation play each other, the player with greater positional knowledge and better chess intuition will usually win. Great chess players like Mikhail Tal frequently came up with creative responses to problems, and often relied entirely on intuition when they couldn't work through all the possibilities in their head. As GM Kasparov says 'it takes more than logic to be a world-class chess player. Intuition is the defining quality of a great chess player'.

By the same token, playing football well isn't just about good positioning, creativity and instinctive reactions, it also requires a lot of calculation. In most situations on the field there is more than one option of what to do at any given moment. Players have to make a quick decision on which one to choose. If a player has moved out of position, do you cover him? Do you play a fast ball up to the strikers or do you play it into space to build up an attack more slowly? Do you overlap the winger or is it too dangerous? The game involves constant calculation - quickly assessing the situation and then making a decision. Football, according to former Dutch international Arnold Muhren, is a game you play 'with your brains, not with your feet'.

In other words, the games are not so different in the way that you play and understand them than it seems at first. If you like playing or watching football you can use the understanding you have to play chess. Similarly, if you are a chess fanatic you will find that your understanding of chess will help you appreciate a good game of football.

An obvious difference between the games is that one is constantly moving whilst the other is static for the most part. However, while many conceive of chess as a slow game, the experience of playing a good game contradicts this. In every static position movement is implied. As long as your mind is constantly thinking through movements and ideas the game will be as alive and exciting as any other sport.

So forget computer games if you want to show off your tactical insight. In many senses, chess gives you the opportunity to play a game of football on a board, controlling every piece and developing your understanding of positioning, movement and combinations with every game you play.

Key for football diagrams:

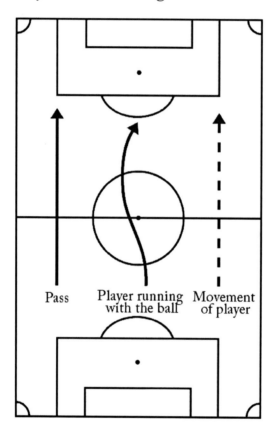

Pass   Player running   Movement
         with the ball   of player

PART 1 - THE TECHNICAL ELEMENTS

Building connections

'Never forget that your pieces should be working as a team! Nurture each and every one of them, make sure they compliment each other.'
Jeremy Silman

To develop play in chess and football you have to build connections between your pieces or players. The way that connections are built between the pieces in chess is similar to the way players build connections on the football field by passing. For instance, if a Rook is placed on a particular file, another piece can connect with it by moving onto a square on that file. The piece is effectively being 'played in' by the Rook in the same way that a midfielder might play a pass through to a striker. To play fluid chess requires strong connections to be built across the board which must be maintained as the game changes and evolves. If the connections are weak, the player will be as helpless as a team who can't retain possession of the ball – unable to develop dangerous attacks.

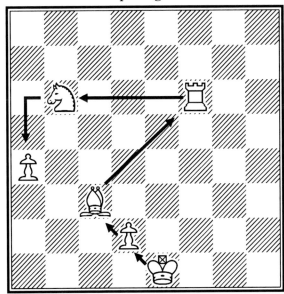

The lines show how the pieces are connected through the way they build off each other.

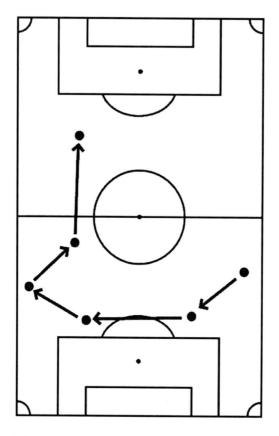

The lines show the way the players are connected through passing the ball to each other.

There are two types of connection to recognise in both games. One is a **direct** connection between pieces or a direct pass to another player. The other is a connection made at a **meeting point** between two players or pieces:

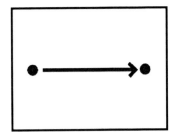 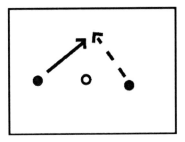

A direct pass

A pass into space on to which the team-mate runs at a meeting point.

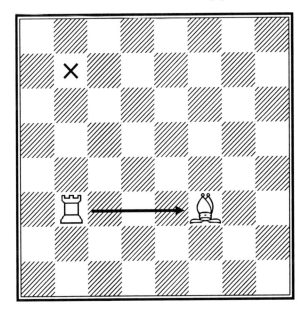

The direct connection between the Rook and the Bishop is shown by the arrow, whilst point X marks the connective meeting point between the two.

Each game is based on **moving** and **connecting**, allowing interplay between pieces or players.

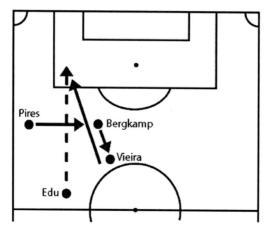

Edu is the fourth man ready to complete the move by running on to the final ball.

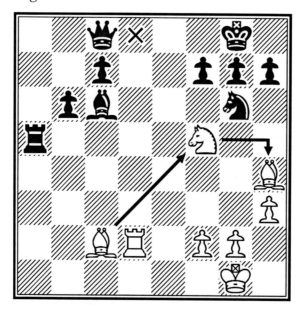

This attack is enabled by the connections built up between the Bishops and the Knight. The Rook waits to move onto the Bishop's line at the meeting point X.

In the examples above, both Edu and the Rook are fairly dormant until they are turned into a threat by the connective work of the players and pieces around them. This can be compared to a line that an artist draws which has no meaning until other lines are drawn around it.

Chess and football are architectural games, and, like any powerfully built edifice, overall strength derives from the underlying structural components. Carefully built, strong connections can lead to a chance at scoring a goal or securing a piece. Successful attacks in football are not reliant solely on the positioning of players or pieces in attacking positions. There must be connective **supply lines** that flow from the back, through the middle, and up to the most attacking players.

In line with the idea of football as an architectural game, coaches often talk about the need for a team to retain their 'shape'. If a team's shape is lost, building connections becomes more difficult because players won't know where to find each other. Chess likewise becomes difficult for the player whose pieces are scattered across the board and unable to interact.

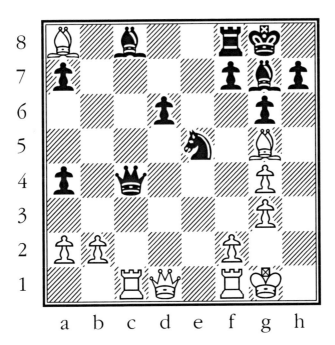

Botvinnik vs Smyslov (1954)

Three White pieces have no direct connection to any other White piece on the board (the pawns on a2 and b2 and the Bishop on a8). Black went on to exploit the confusion and win.

DOMINATING THE MIDFIELD

'A strong midfield counts for 60 to 70 per cent of the game'
Claudio Ranieri

To control a game of chess, it is important to dominate the middle of the board. The reason is simple – it gives you the most options to develop your attacks. As Nigel Short says, 'if you control the centre you dominate the board'. The pieces controlling the middle can 'play in' other pieces which build off them on either side of the board. Pawns are very good at supporting stronger pieces from the centre. Likewise in football, if your midfield can control the game, other players can move into attacking positions. At the same time, your opponent will not have so many possibilities to build their own attacks. Controlling the middle of the board should be the chess player's first priority.

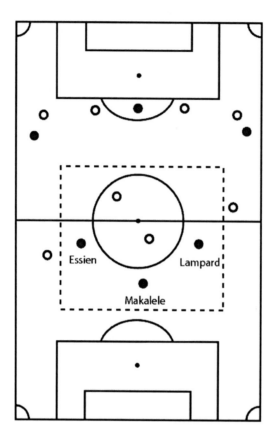

Chelsea use a close-nit three man midfield in an attempt to dominate against a team playing a traditional 4-4-2 formation.

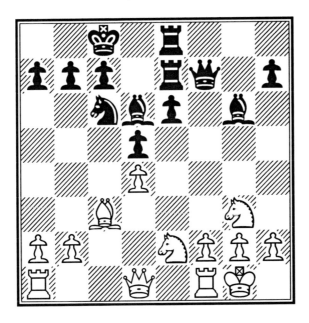

Although Black offers no immediate threat, its pieces are better placed to gain control of the central area of the board.

Football coaches often place their most aggressive players in this area. There are many examples of midfielders who have made their name as much through their aggression as their skill with the ball. Roy Keane was cited by Alex Ferguson as the best player he ever had at Manchester United. Despite not having the technical qualities of many team-mates over the years, his ferocious desire to win the midfield battle in many games was seen by Ferguson as the single most important factor in his teams' success.

Chess may not be a physical contest, but the mental aggression required to win games should not be underestimated. As Emmanuel Lasker said, 'chess is above all a fight' - and it is the middle of the board where the most intense fighting takes place. At the beginning of a game the pieces battle to stake their claim to this ground in much the same way that footballers try to establish their midfield superiority as soon as the match begins. Like animals claiming territory, the players that lose out at the beginning often don't recover for the rest of the game.

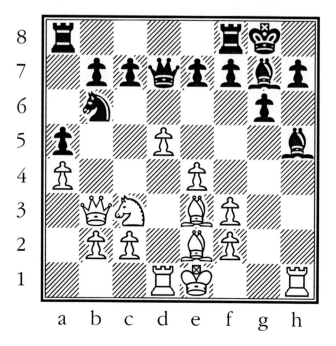

Smyslov vs Botvinnik (1958)

Smyslov occupies two of the central four squares as well as having reinforcements from the more powerful pieces which, apart from the h1 Rook, are all centrally placed.

Build-up Play

' Some players get a few pieces out and launch an attack. The correct way to play chess is to develop each and every piece. Chess is a team game!'
Jeremy Silman

The great Dutch football coach, Renus Michels, breaks down the attacking process in football into three components:

- 'organisational guidelines' (overall structure)
- 'strategic guidelines' (general plans)
- 'tactical guidelines' (specific plans).

In this way he is clarifying the need for a football team to have a basic structure to begin with, a general idea of how they are going to build attacks, and a very specific idea of how to execute a particular attack. The organisational guidelines will have direct implications for the strategy, and the strategy will have a direct influence on how attacks are executed tactically.

This process is almost identical to that of a Grandmaster's when building and executing an attack in chess. The opening that he chooses will, to a large extent, dictate the shape of the game, and affect strategic and tactical decisions that he makes later.

	CHESS
ORGANISATIONAL SYSTEM	Choice of opening (Ruy Lopez), (Sicilian Defence) etc…
STRATEGIC CONSIDERATIONS IN BUILD-UP PHASE	➤ Take the initiative or counter-attack? ➤ Tempo ➤ Identifying weak spots in the opposition ➤ Attack down centre or wings? ➤ Structure
SPECIFIC TACTICAL CONSIDERATIONS IN ATTACKING PHASE	➤ Attacking combinations ➤ Making breakthroughs and capturing pieces

In chess terminology, there are principally two types of move. Moves that are made for long-term reasons, without an immediate goal in mind, are known as **strategic** or **positional** moves. These are found in the build-up phase and are chosen as part of the overall strategy. Moves that are precisely calculated, with specific goals in mind, are known as **tactical** moves. These are found in the attacking phase.

FOOTBALL

Formations
(4-4-2), (4-3-3)
(5-3-2), (3-1-3-3) etc…

- ➤ Take the initiative or counter-attack?
- ➤ Type of build-up play
- ➤ Identifying weak spots in
  the opposition
- ➤ Attack down centre or wings?
- ➤ Structure

- ➤ Attacking combinations
- ➤ Making breakthroughs and creating
  scoring chances

In football terminology, 'tactics' tends to be used as an umbrella term for strategic and tactical moves. This is perhaps too general. There are many chess players who are strategically strong but tactically weak. The situation is the same in football, but the language of football does not allow this to be expressed very clearly.

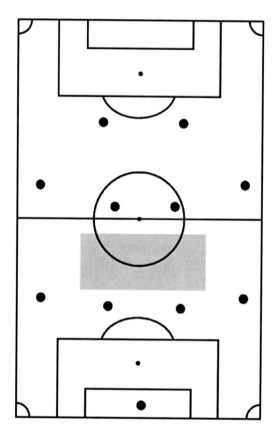

The 4-4-2 formation offers a lot of possibilities for attacking down the wings, and so the team strategy will involve getting the ball to the wingers regularly and building attacks from there. One of the main weaknesses is the vacant space between midfield and defence which can be exploited by the opposition.

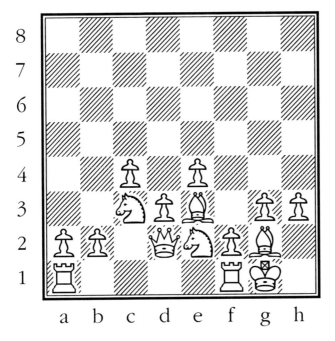

The 'Botvinnik formation' is nicely balanced and offers possibilities of developing the pawns on b2 or f2, depending on which side the player wants to focus his attack. White's strategy will be to build an attack from the d5 square, which is well supported by the two pawns at the front. However, the d4 square is a weakness which the opponent will try to exploit.

Each organisational system will have its strong and weak points. The strategy must make the best use of the strongest aspects of the system.

Once the strategic plan has been chosen, players must start the build-up process in accordance with this plan. In chess this must include good **development of pieces**. This means activating as many pieces as possible in the opening. It is very tempting to try to gain an advantage by attacking quickly. Continually bringing out pieces can seem like a waste of attacking momentum. However, very few successful attacks can be launched without proper piece development. Only then will there be sufficient options for interplay amongst the pieces to perform well in the attacking phase. If you attack without developing your pieces fully, it must be executed perfectly because there will be no backup if the attack is foiled.

The same is true for attacking play in football. You cannot just leave it to your strikers to do the attacking. There must be support from the midfielders and defenders to enable more options. Teams are often afraid to bring extra players into an attacking move for fear of losing the momentum. However, while some momentum may be lost in the short term, when it comes to moving in for the kill, it may prove to have been fruitful. Manchester United, under Alex Ferguson, have mastered this, finding a good balance between careful player development and retaining momentum.

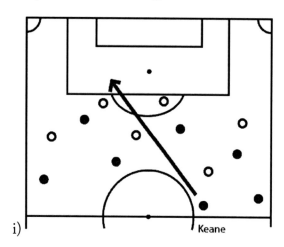

i)   Keane

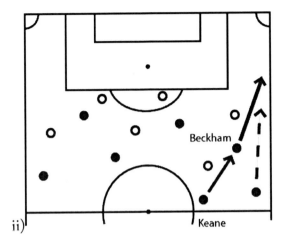

ii) Beckham Keane

Keane ignores the option of playing it to the strikers quickly (i) and instead plays it wide to Beckham (ii). Beckham also decides not to play the attacking ball into the strikers but plays it through to Neville who is overloading on the right hand side.

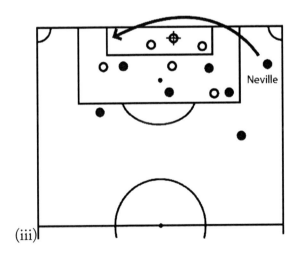

Neville

(iii)

When the cross finally comes in from Neville there are lots of players waiting for the ball in the box making it much easier for the strikers to score (iii).

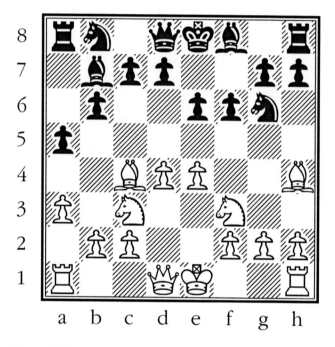

Here White is better placed to develop a powerful attack because it has four of its stronger pieces developed whilst Black only has two.

Another important decision to be made by a coach or chess player in the build-up phase is where to focus the attack. There are three main attacking outlets on the board or the pitch: the left wing, the right wing and the centre. The decision will naturally be influenced by the defensive set up of the opponent. Often a defense will close off certain areas more than others.

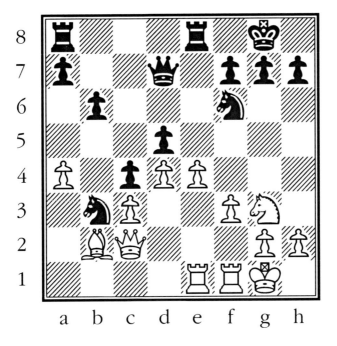

Botvinnik vs Capablanca (1938)

White has neglected to defend the pawn on a4 and instead chosen to advance his e-pawn to e4. By doing this he is inviting Black to attack down his left side so that he will have the possibility of attacking through the centre. Black duly took the pawn on a4, making it a question of whether Black's attack on the left would prevail over White's attack down the centre. In the end White powered through on the e-file to win the game.

For teams playing a counter-attacking style, the nature of build-up play is different. Their strategy is to invite opponents to attack them and pounce on the defensive weaknesses they leave behind. For this reason their attacks are direct and high-tempo, but occur very infrequently. GM Karpov used this strategy, as do many Italian coaches.

MOBILITY

'I don't think formations matter...our true formation was movement'
Arrigo Sacchi

An important requirement for retaining possession in football is the availability of passing options for a player who has the ball. Great teams like Manchester United often have three or four good passing options each time a player has the ball. This is made possible by the mobility of the players who are making runs without the ball. If players are static, the number of **options** is cut down dramatically, and building connections through passing becomes more difficult.

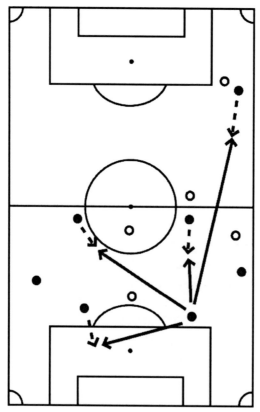

Here the central defender has many options because four players have dropped into space to receive the ball.

The same concept applies to the chess pieces. Tarrasch was the first grandmaster to emphasise the importance of mobility and he demonstrated its value in many of his games. His belief was that good mobility improves a player's options, which allows them to hold the initiative more easily.

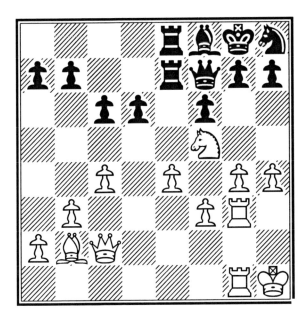

Tarrasch vs Schlecter (1894)

To have good mobility in chess, your pieces must have space in which they can move. Here Tarrasch's pieces are well spread out with various options for movement. Black, in contrast, are clustered together and unable to move freely. Tarrasch converted this extra mobility into an easy win.

As the different chess pieces have different types of movement, the connective possibilities between them are consequently extremely varied and complex. It is perhaps not surprising that modern football has taken something from this: players now realise that through varying their movements, more complicated possibilities for interplay with team-mates can arise. In fact, to a large extent, they mimic the movements of pieces on a chess board. For instance, modern players often make diagonal runs (mimicking the movement of a Bishop) or change direction in the middle of a run (mimicking the movement of a Knight).

PIECE POSITIONS

There are particular values which chess pieces have been given. For instance, a pawn is considered to be worth 1 point, a Knight 3 and a Rook 5. These provide us with a useful tool for evaluating the strength of our positions in a game. However, as most chess players know, it is not enough to give static values to pieces. A pawn can be more powerful than a Rook if it is used in the right way, just as a Rook used in the wrong way can be completely useless. The truth is that pieces only have a value according to how they are behaving in a particular situation.

Since every game of chess is different, there can be no definite right or wrong for where pieces should and shouldn't be placed. However, just as players are better suited to certain positions in football, chess pieces will likewise normally have more influence when placed on particular parts of the board. Roberto Carlos, for instance, will run up and down the left wing for the whole game, dominating that space. A Rook can do a similar thing on the chess board when the game has opened up. However, when either are placed in the centre of the action where there is less space, they are far less likely to be effective. A Knight is generally more dangerous in the centre of the board because it has more options from there. Its awkward movements and ability to jump over other pieces make it difficult to defend against in tight situations. If it is stuck on the wing it normally has very little influence because it is slow. Similarly, the influence of a player like Paul Scholes would be greatly diminished if he was playing on the wing. His clever movement makes him difficult to contain and his sharp awareness means he can influence everything around him.

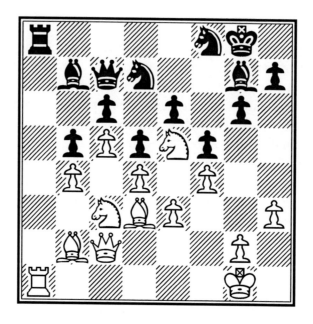

Bronstein vs Botvinnik (1951)

The game is very congested in the middle of the board, which is why the Knights are in more central areas. The only space is on the left wing where the Rooks are more suited.

If your pieces are in their most effective positions this can offer a huge advantage in terms of attacking potential, even if you are down in material.

Although Black has material advantage, the White pieces are placed in far more useful positions. The Knights are attacking several squares and the Rooks are dominating the central d-file. Meanwhile Black's Rooks are fairly immobile, the Knights are stuck on the wings, and the Bishop is trapped behind the Rook.

USING SPACE

One of the first instructions young footballers receive from a coach while they are playing a game is 'use the space'. It is important that footballers and chess players consciously think about space from an early age. What does it mean to 'use the space'? For the footballer and the chess player it means to identify the vacant space and exploit it.

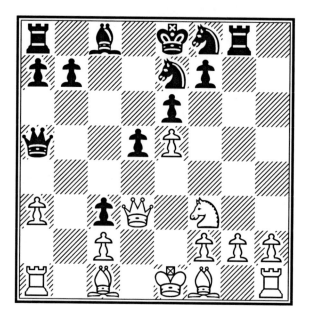

Smyslov vs Botvinnik (1954)

Smyslov has cleverly opened up a lot of space on the right wing. His game plan from here on is to attack this space with his pawns.

Finally, when the pawn has reached h6 (below) Botvinnik resigns.

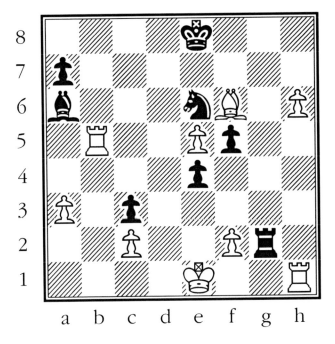

In football, the player with the ball will often choose a pass based on who has the most space. Beckham passes to Giggs (overleaf) on this basis.

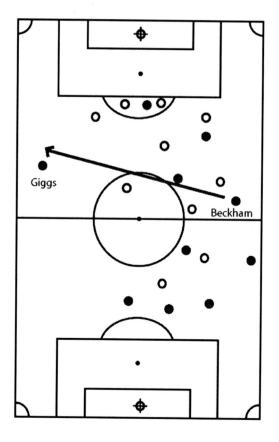

In chess you are given all the tools you need to use all the
space on the board effectively. Bishops can be used to exploit
open diagonal files; Rooks can do the same for straight files;
Knights are tailored towards more tight situations. In football,
coaches try to build a team where different players will be able
to meet the demands of the various positions of the pitch,
to use the space most effectively. It is not just a question of
moving players or pieces into the vacant space, but of having
a range of connective potential to extend into that space.

For instance, Xabi Alonso gives Liverpool the possibility of using the full depth and width of the field because he can pass over huge distances with great accuracy. Thus, a winger can go very wide, knowing that he can still receive the ball from Alonso.

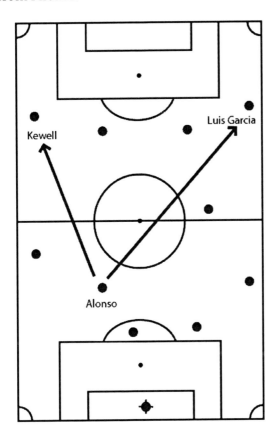

Likewise, with its long range of connectivity, the Bishop can sit deep and support attacks on both sides of the board.

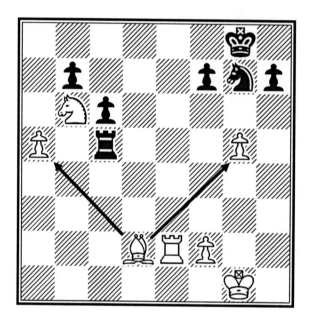

CREATING SPACE

'The main problem I had to solve when my players were in possession of the ball was the one of creating space: searching for, creating and occupying space in the different parts of the field, and exploiting that space in an effective and positive way'
Giovanni Trappatoni

In football and chess there is a constant need to open up space, especially at the highest levels where defences are more organised and space is not given away cheaply. It is not enough to wait for gaps to appear because often they won't.

It was in the 1970s that Renus Michels, coach of Ajax, and Johan Cruyff, his most important player, started to think about space differently. As the coach Dave Sexton says, 'with their pressing and rotation the Dutch created space where there wasn't any before. Everyone else still played in a rigid way, in straight lines and fixed positions'. In the eyes of many admirers Michels and Cruyff were like chess players. Bobby Haarms, for instance, described Michels as 'like a chess master of football tactics'. As well he might, for the Dutch coach was taking tactical ideas fundamental to chess and applying them to football.

One technique that Cruyff talked about was that of dragging defenders out of their positions. Once the defender is lured out of position, space is opened up in the area that he was occupying. This tactic has been used in chess for many centuries and has now become a standard part of a football player's tactical knowledge.

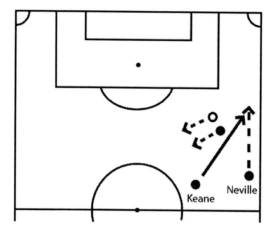

The right winger cuts inside, encouraging the full back to follow him. This leaves Neville to come into the space that has been left vacant, and Keane passes to him.

In chess this is called **deflecting** pieces. You force a defensive piece away from a certain spot so that the space that it occupied can be exploited.

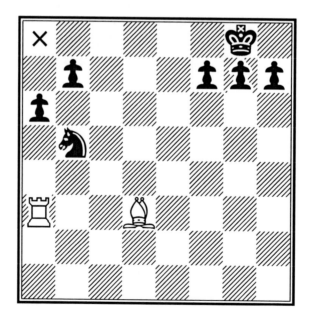

White wants to move the Rook to point X. The Bishop takes the Knight, prompting the pawn to capture the Bishop. This leaves the Rook with an open file so that he is free to move down the a-file.

Tal vs Benko (1964)

Tal wants to attack the pawn on f7 with his Knight but he can't because the King is defending it. He moves his Rook from d1 to d8, encouraging the Black King to take it, so that his Knight will be free to move. Deflecting the King in this way will win him the Queen.

Apart from deflecting defenders, you can move a piece in order to unleash the attacking threat of a piece directly behind. This is called a **discovered** attack. Such attacks are common because defences normally concentrate on the first line of attack and neglect the second wave.

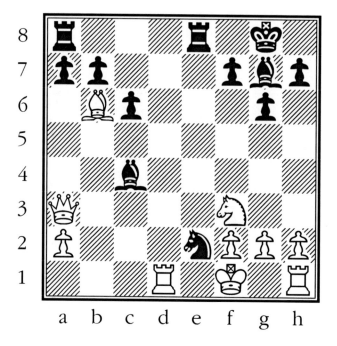

Byrne vs Fischer (1956)

The Black Knight moves to c3 allowing the Bishop to attack the King. The Knight can then take the White Rook because the King must move (as it is in check).

In football, a similar thing frequently happens. This is why midfielders making late runs, like Paul Scholes and Frank Lampard, score so many goals.

This principle does not just apply to pieces in attacking positions, it can apply to pieces anywhere on the board. For instance, a pawn moving out from the start position is not just useful in itself but also because it is opening space for the pieces behind it.

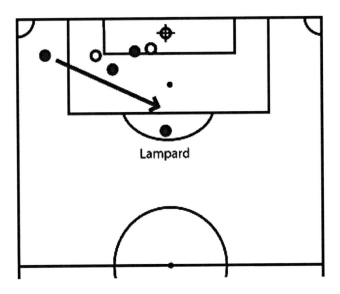

Chelsea vs Fulham (2005)

The first line of attackers deflect the defenders away from Lampard who is making a run behind. The ball comes in and Lampard scores.

EXPLOITING WEAKNESSES

'A successful attack is nothing more than the correct exploitation of (exploitable) weakness'
Andrew Soltis

The key to winning in football and chess is in finding the opponents defensive weaknesses and exploiting them. Identifying weaknesses is often difficult and can require a lot of insight. It is in this capacity that top level football coaches, with good analytical abilities, can have a large effect on a game. With each individual move during a game, something in the overall structure will become stronger and something weaker. For instance, a chess piece moving into an attacking position will probably have left a defensive weakness behind. Likewise, in football, if a full back makes an overlapping run, the team will be defensively weak down that side. If the opposition regain possession they will try to attack that momentary weakness. It is important for players to be able to recognise this dynamic throughout games so that fleeting weaknesses can be exploited. If a chess player or coach can notice a more long term vulnerability, they will make this a 'pressure point', and probe away at it.

It is equally important to find opponents' *attacking* weaknesses. This prevents the problem of overdefending. It is inefficient to commit anything more to defence than is absolutely necessary, as Steinitz suggests in his principle of economy. If the opponent is unable to exploit a weak spot, there is no need to defend it.

England coach Sven Goran Erikkson correctly replaced Jamie Carragher in the 2006 World Cup game against Trinidad and Tobago because England were overdefending on their right flank.

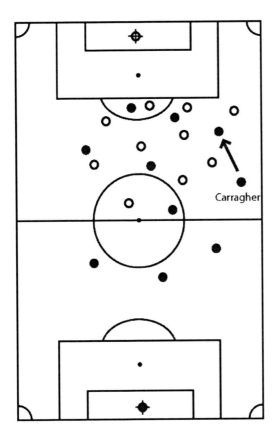

Carragher plays the ball to Beckham who is not using the full width of the field. On several occasions in the first half Beckham was pressed and returned the ball to Carragher to cross it. This was not an ideal situation because Carragher is not particularly skilled at crossing the ball.

In the second half, Trinidad offered no threat to Carragher down England's right side. Erikkson took off Carragher and played Beckham in his role. Beckham's lack of defensive ability was unlikely to be exploited. In place of Carragher came Aaron Lennon who posed a far greater attacking threat.

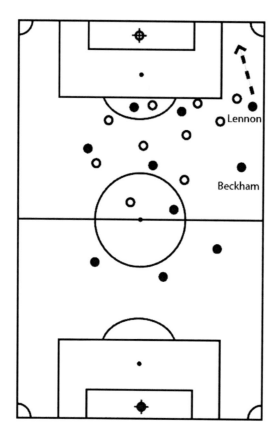

Here Lennon is using the full width of the field, dragging more defenders wide with him. When pressed Lennon passed the ball back to Beckham who provided crosses from the right back position. Indeed, it was a cross from Beckham that finally broke down the defence and enabled England to score.

Such a game proved how big a factor tactics play in football. The superior abilities of the England players made little difference for most of the game because Trinidad were tactically superior. It was only through Erikkson's changes that England were able to create a breakthrough.

Another game which demonstrated a coach's ability to identify and exploit weaknesses in the opposition was Chelsea's 2005 Champions League match against Barcelona. At the time, Barcelona were arguably the best club team in the world.

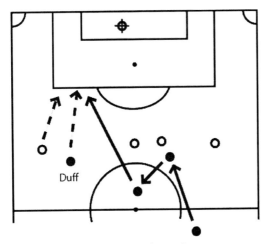

Chelsea vs Barcelona (2005)

Barcelona started the game boldly with their defence pushed high up the field, and with large gaps between their defenders. However, this meant they were vulnerable to counter-attacks. Mourinho had prepared Chelsea for this beforehand, and they exploited the weakness by counter-attacking very quickly from the beginning of the game. Within 25 minutes they were 3-0 up.

In the following game, White exploits a large hole in the opposition defence.

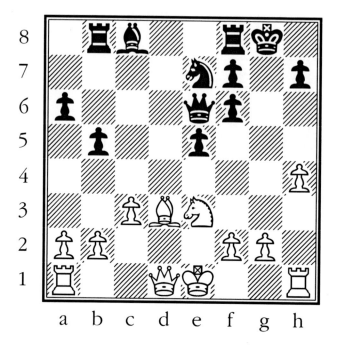

Kasparov vs Lautier (1994)

Black has held his own well enough but the lack of a pawn in front of the King on g7 is a potential weak spot which Kasparov goes on to exploit by attacking with his Queen, Rook and the pawn on the right wing:

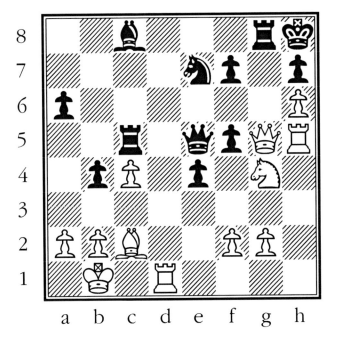

At this point Black resigns because he sees checkmate on the horizon with any number of combinations.

Sometimes the weaknesses are more subtle than an obvious hole in the defence.

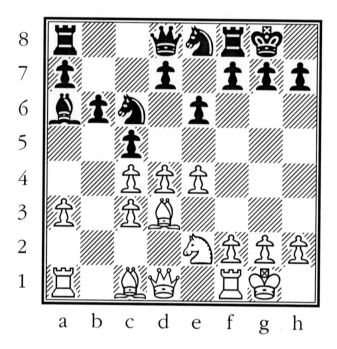

Geller vs Smyslov (1953)

In an analysis of this game, Garry Kasparov reveals how Black identifies the weakness of White as being the pawn on c4 (since this pawn can't be defended by any other pawn). His long term plan is to destabilise White by attacking this piece. White identifies Black's weakness as the lack of defence on Black's left side, and focuses his attacking plans on this area.

Stretching the Defence

One of the most common ways to lose a piece is by leaving a defensive piece with too much to do. It may, for instance, be protecting two or three other pieces simultaneously. In some situations this can be a good arrangement. Provided the pieces are not under direct threat, it is an efficient and flexible way to defend, allowing other pieces to concentrate on attacking duties. However, if two of the pieces are suddenly threatened at same time, one will be lost because the defensive piece has become **overloaded**.

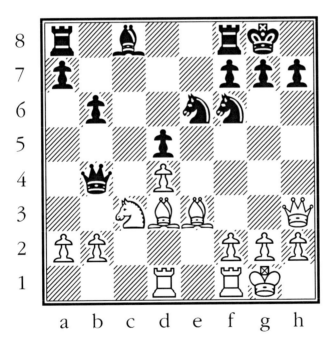

Moiseenko vs Savchenko (2006)

Black is in the unfortunate situation of relying on the f6 Knight to defend the pawn in the centre *and* the pawn on h7. Since the priority is to defend the pawn on h7 (Queen x h7 is instant checkmate) the White Knight safely takes the central Black pawn.

This is the equivalent of one footballer being in charge of marking two attacking players. As long as the two players aren't getting the ball it is efficient. Once they do, however, it will be two against one and difficult to defend against.

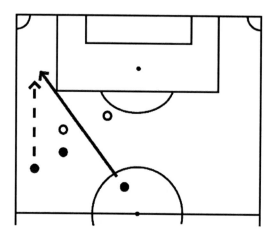

The point of overlapping in football is to force the defenders into an **overload** situation. Here the full back overlaps on the left wing, leaving the defender facing two attacking players by himself.

COMBINATIONS

'To conceive combinations and execute them properly requires originality, imagination, insight. Above all, it requires that quality, common to great artists, scientists, and statesmen, of seizing a number of apparently disparate elements and combining them into a harmonious unit'

Philip W. Sergeant

Combinations are generally used in the attacking phase of chess and football, and constitute one of the most exciting aspects of the games. A situation that may be regarded as a combination is one in which at least 2 players or pieces interplay in a single move, normally over a small area, to break down a defence or gain some advantage. The idea is that the combination is so clever that it can't be defended against. They often involve the use of **deflections, discovered attacks** and **overloads**. Successfully executed combinations are one of the most satisfying elements of both games.

The execution of a good combination in chess requires an ability to calculate. Calculation involves working through the possibilities of movements and connections between pieces. Whilst footballers are clearly not required to have the calculation capabilities of a professional chess player, it is nonetheless important for them to have some capacity to think ahead. This allows them to stay one step ahead of defenders and judge when an attack can be realised. As in chess, combinations consist of movements and connections (passes). The international footballer Arnold Muhren saw these calculations as an essential part of the game: 'It's a thinking game. It's not running around everywhere and just working hard.... Before I had the ball I knew exactly what to do with it. I always knew two or three moves ahead.'

Coaches of chess and football tend to concentrate on

the build-up phase in training sessions. In this way they can convey general rules of positional play and strategy which can be implemented by players relatively quickly. The attacking phase is more difficult to coach because it is not governed by rules to the same extent. Players are presented with a different situation each time they enter this phase and must come up with an original idea to find the solution for the particular problem. So whilst defensive organisation and build-up play can be coached to a large extent, coaches are often reliant on attacking players to use their own insight and creativity to solve the specific problems of the attacking phase. This is one of the reasons why football coaches are likely to spend more money on attacking players than defensive ones. It is possible to develop ability with continual practice, but players must already possess a large degree of natural insight to be effective in the attacking phase. Combinations are a part of the games in which the genuinely talented excel.

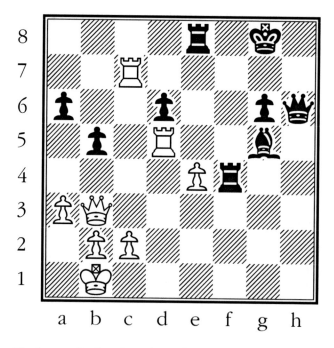

Fischer vs Bolbochan (1962)

Fischer's King may be under pressure soon from Black's Rook, Bishop and Queen. However, this isn't a problem as he works out a combination with his Queen and Rooks to check-mate Black quickly. First he moves his Rook to e5. This means the Black King is in check (from the White Queen). The King moves to f8 to defend the Rook next to it.

Fischer then takes the f7 Rook with his own Rook, and the Black King completes the swap:

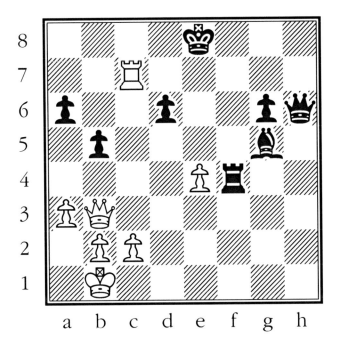

The Black King is put in check by the White Queen moving to e6, and Fischer proceeds to put the King in check again after it moves to f8. The Bishop moves down to defend but the Queen just takes it and it is check mate. An unstoppable winning combination.

Arsenal, under Arsene Wenger, have mastered the art of combination play and have probably scored more goals through combinations than any other team in top level world football.

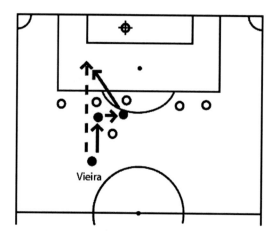

Vieira

Here Arsenal slice open Liverpool's defence with a slick combination in which Vieira plays the ball forward whilst making a forward run. The ball is played between two Arsenal attackers before it is returned to Vieira in the box. He slots the ball into the net.

Combinations in football are difficult because they require a group of players to be thinking as one. While the chess player is in total control of his pieces, a footballer needs his teammates to understand his intentions. If players fully understand the system they are playing, they will have a greater ability to think ahead as a group, anticipating the movements and passes of other players. In this sense the coach is the chessmaster and must train the players to execute his personal vision of how to play. Although he cannot control exactly what players do on the pitch, he can develop a system which players can understand and follow. This explains why top-level coaches like Arsene Wenger and Jose Mourinho have built teams with different players that nevertheless play in a very similar way. Players must have the tactical insight to carry out the coach's plans. It is a two-way process between coach and player, and if one is lacking, the other must make up for it.

DEFENDING

'Mourinho possesses the acute spatial sense of a chess grandmaster. They defend as one, all pieces supporting each other, and when they attack they do so decisively.'
Will Buckley

In Jose Mourinho's first season at Chelsea, the defence he fashioned was so strong that his team conceded a mere 15 goals in a complete season of 38 Premiership games. Over the course of the season, they provided a model of correct defending that all footballers and chess players should aspire to. This extraordinary record was achieved by mastering principles that Lasker describes in his 'Manual of Chess'. Lasker's two major principles of defending, as originally proposed by Steinitz, are a) efficiency and b) maintaining equal strength across the line of defence.

Efficient defending involves avoiding inhibiting each other. Players and pieces can be stifled as much by their own side as by the opposition. A poor chess player might, for instance, have his Bishop trapped behind his Knight, reducing a potentially powerful piece to near insignificance. This is like having three players marking one man. Secondly, each piece must be doing more than one thing. For instance the Knight may be protecting up to three pieces at once; the Bishop may be defending a piece and attacking a file at the same time. A left back must be aware of the threat of the striker on the inside right channel. On top of this he must be alert to the threat of the overlap from the full back. If he's worrying too much about the overlap then the central defenders may get into trouble.

The most important aspect of defensive efficiency is the detection and correction of over-defending. Any defence must be run like the most streamlined of businesses: never should two people be left to idly perform a task that can be adequately carried out by one. The extra person must be deployed where he can be more useful. As Steinitz himself put it, players must "make the least concession that just suffices, not an ounce more, not the dot of an 'i' too much". Only by defending with absolute efficiency can any chess player or football team begin to master the second principle: that of maintaining equal strength across the lines.

As games progress, the dynamics of attack and defense change. Weak spots shift from one area to the next. An area that is solidly defended at one moment can become weakened suddenly because of a change in the opposition. Players must be able to adapt fluidly to these changes. New defensive weaknesses will continually spring up, and good defenses will patch them up immediately, whether they are under immediate threat or not. By maintaining equal strength across defensive lines, to the maximum degree to which this is realistically possible, weaknesses can be kept to a minimum.

One could argue that zonal defending is the most effective because it is the most efficient. In chess, good defending involves an understanding of how to defend areas of the board rather than just particular squares or pieces. As Dr Colin Crouch says, 'the prophylactic player would be thinking in terms of complexes of squares here, and not just single squares'.

The **prophylactic** method that Crouch refers to is a style of defending that involves stopping attacks before they even have a chance to begin. Perhaps the most famous chess player to use this technique was Karpov. Opponents of Karpov often got frustrated because they couldn't get into the danger areas to start causing him any problems. Often they ran out of ideas or else made a mistake out of frustration. At this point Karpov would launch a counter-attack.

A great example of the way Karpov was happy to wait patiently and soak up the pressure is his game against Pablo Ricardi.

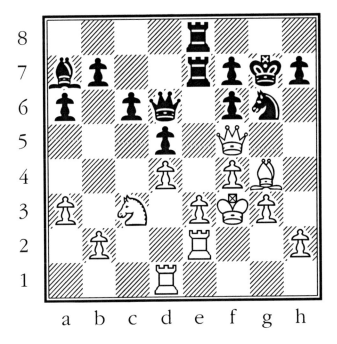

Karpov vs Ricardi (2001)

Up to this point Karpov has stifled any attacking options except those on the Black's right wing. Ricardi sees it as his only option to attack on this side and so he brings his pawn to b5. Black makes some headway from an attacking point of view...

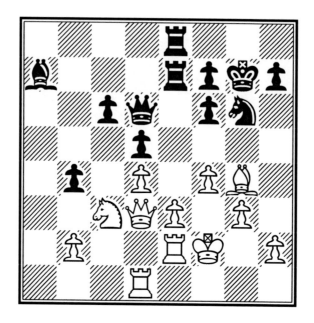

... but Karpov is prepared for this.

In the next few moves Black tries to keep up the pressure with advances from his Rook and Queen. However, because the defense is so tight, these are feeble attempts at hurting Karpov and he continues to drive Ricardi's pieces away. Once Black has run out of attacking ideas Karpov picks him off with a vicious counter attack on White's left flank mobilising his Knight, Rook and Queen:

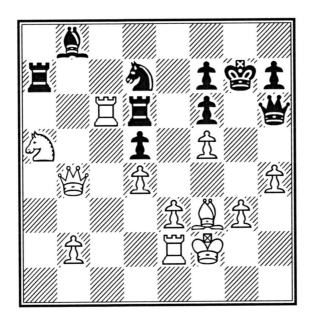

At this point Ricardi resigns.

This whole game by Karpov seems to follow perfectly the blueprint laid out for a counter-attacking style of football by the Dutch coach Rinus Michels. Michels does not call it 'prophylaxis' but the principles are essentially the same. For him, it is important for a team playing this style of football that 'coherence between the defenders is optimal. In that manner, you can close down the operational attacking space of the opponents'. Thus, it is about closing down the attacking *space* rather than the actual attacks. In other words, attacks are stopped before they have even begun. Michels says that this style of play involves 'letting the opponents keep the initiative of the game.' Of course, this is exactly what Karpov does in his game against Ricardi, allowing his opponent to attack him. Michels continues, 'a good counter attack team needs to have a strong defensive line with players who will remain calm even under high pressure'. Karpov was famed for his ability to remain composed and defensively solid under immense attacking pressure. And the purpose of this, according to Michels? 'To take advantage of the space behind their defense.' Again, exactly as Karpov does against Ricardi once the pawns have moved forward and left space behind.

The Italian national team have traditionally played a prophylactic game. Such is their defensive organisation all over the field that teams are often incapable of creating any chances, let alone scoring against them. Like Karpov, Italy are organised to stop attacks before they have even started. Once a weakness is spotted in the opposition, it is swiftly and ruthlessly exploited.

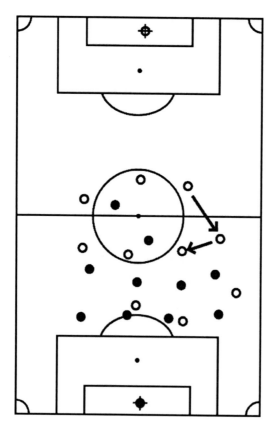

Here the Italian team sit deep, making sure there are no gaps in their defence. They allow the opponent to have the ball and attack them.

The moment the opposition attack disintegrates, a fast counter-attack is launched, in a typically Karpovian manner. The midfielders immediately play the ball up to the strikers who try to exploit the large amount of space behind the defence.

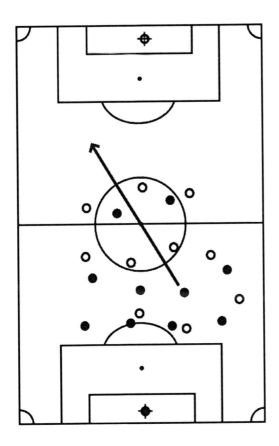

STRETCH AND COMPRESS

It is far easier to attack in chess and football if there is a lot of free space. By extension, defending involves closing down the space as much as possible. To this end, in attacking situations players or pieces tend to be spread out more, whilst in defensive situations they are closer together. Given that there is a need to balance attack and defense during games, a team that is attacking needs to have an idea of how it will quickly close down the space if it loses the ball. Similarly, once a team has defended an attack, it should know how to spread out and open up the playing space.

The great Ajax teams had the ability to stretch and compress very efficiently. When they lost the ball they would contract and press so well as a unit that they won the ball back quickly. This saved them energy and time, and kept them in control of the game. Such a tactic is very difficult to execute because it means everyone has to be aware of everyone else to keep the shape of the team. This is a common trait in Dutch football as a whole, and has been recognisable in the national team for many years. The Dutch international Ruud Krol explains, 'When we were defending, the gaps between us had to be very short. When we attacked, we spread out and used the wings. When we defended, we looked to keep the opponent on the half way line. You don't want to run back to defend because you are trying to save energy'. This tactic requires a great deal of understanding between the players.

On the chess board you have to have your pieces positioned so that they can do the same thing. Mobility is very important for this reason. Switching smoothly between attack and defence is crucial for any football team or chess player. From an aesthetic point of view, teams that can contract and spread out effectively are 'breathing' smoothly and are nicer to watch. Manchester United, under Alex Ferguson, are a good example of a team who contract well as a unit and then spread out as a unit once they've won the ball back. They never contract too much or spread too quickly.

Likewise, in Euro 2000 the Dutch national team were notable for their mastery of this technique.

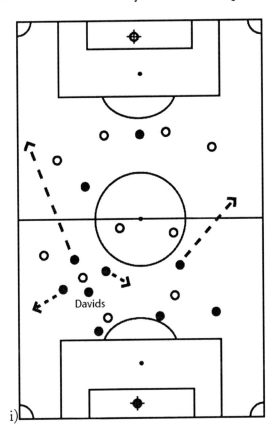

i)

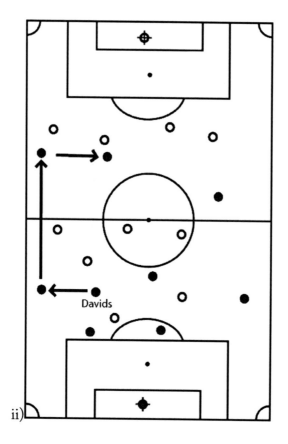

Holland (2000)

Four Dutch players compress (i), surrounding the opposition player with the ball, which helps Davids to win back possession. Once possession is regained, the team spread using the whole pitch (ii).

PRESSING

Pressing in football or chess involves putting pressure on the attacking players or pieces by stopping their advance. It is important to know when and how to press. Players must find a balance between pressing too hard and letting the opposition overrun them. In football, pressing the opponents defence whenever they have the ball can be an effective way of snuffing out any attacking threat at an early stage. However, this tactic requires a lot of energy that could potentially be used more productively elsewhere. On top of this, one good pass into midfield can bypass all the pressure.

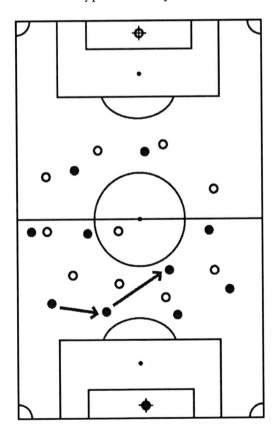

The defender passes to the midfielder, by-passing four players in the opposition who are pressing high up the field.

In chess, it is sometimes tempting to pin back a piece that has moved into an attacking position just for the peace of mind. However, it may turn out that forcing the opponent's piece to retreat has left you in more danger because your defensive pieces have been drawn out too much.

These problems with pressing hard high up the field have convinced many teams not to press until the attack has entered deeper into their defensive lines.

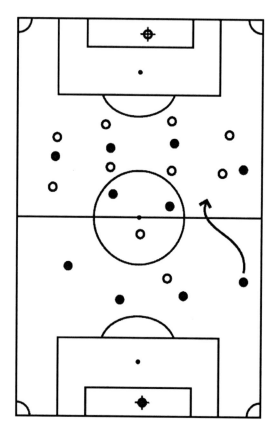

Here the right back is advancing with the ball. Instead of trying to stop him, the two lines of four defenders allow him to do this. It is only when he reaches the first line that the defense will press. To play this type of defence effectively you have to be very good at intercepting passes and choosing the perfect moment to move in for a tackle.

Exerting defensive pressure does not simply involve trying to capture a piece or trying to win the ball back, it often just involves blocking and threatening. The different types of pressing are demonstrated below.

Blocking

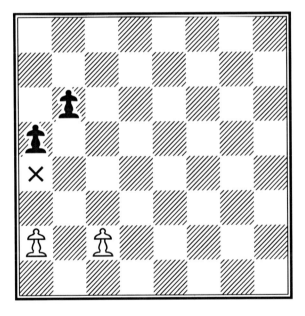

The White pawn on a2 moves forward to stop the advance of the Black pawn on the a-file.

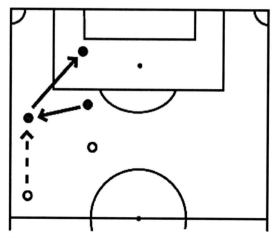

The left winger pressurises the right back by blocking his advance and the ball is played back to the goalkeeper. The player exerting the pressure is not expected to make a tackle, only to block any advance.

Cutting out the options

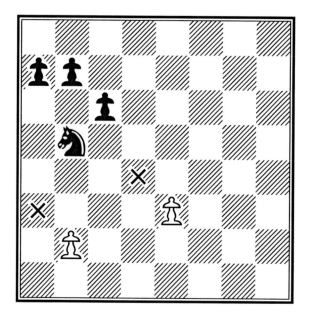

Here White doesn't threaten the Knight itself but exerts pressure by stopping it from moving onto the squares marked X.

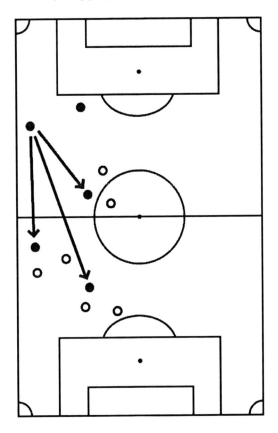

Instead of pressuring the right back himself, this time the defending team press the players to whom he may pass.

Direct threats

In more serious situations, more intense pressure has to be applied.

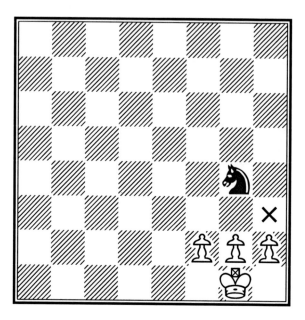

White cannot allow the Knight to sit in such a dangerous area and so makes a direct threat to it by moving its pawn on the h-file to point X. Black must either move his Knight or risk losing it in the next move.

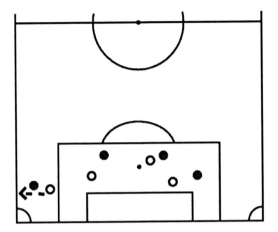

The left-back knows he cannot allow the right winger to cross the ball and so makes a direct threat in the form of a tackle. The attacking player must either evade the challenge or lose the ball.

Defending is not just a reactive discipline. The way a team exerts pressure will determine the scope and limit of the opposition's attacking potentials. Thus if you feel the main attacking threat comes from your opponents left side, you can focus more energy on pressing this side so that they are forced to attack down the other side. A shrewd defense will neutralise the most powerful players in the opposition and shut off the most dangerous attacking channels.

ROTATING

Patience is a necessity for chess players and footballers. The better players have shown that the urge to attempt an attacking breakthrough with sheer force should be resisted. Even in a losing situation, it is better to wait for openings to arrive. For many teams, the process of waiting for this moment involves the tactic of rotating the ball. Chelsea, under Jose Mourinho, are a good example of this.

This is a relatively new idea in English football. The old school of thought held that when a full-back received the ball he should pass it up the field, maintaining the attacking momentum:

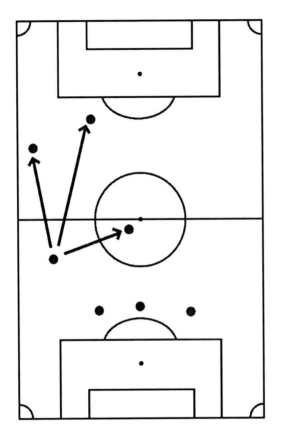

Under Mourinho, if the full-back has no good options for a forward pass, he is instructed to rotate the ball back across to the right back (overleaf). Whilst the tempo is slower, this method allows the team to have more control over when and how their attack will develop.

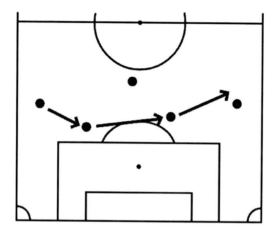

As a general rule, one does not want to surrender an attacking situation by rotating. For instance, if a winger has the ball and can cross it, normally he will do so, or at least be expected to. In chess, it would make sense to keep going forward, unless you are forced to retreat, as to lose ground is to lose some of the initiative. However, among the top teams and top players there are many instances where rotating has proved to be a good attacking move. For instance, the Ajax team under Louis Van Gaal used to switch the ball across the field if the wingers were facing two defenders. The idea was that there must be a free man on the other side of the field if two defenders were marking the winger with the ball. Of course, the rotation has to be executed with great speed and precision because the opposition would normally have time to reorganise their defence.

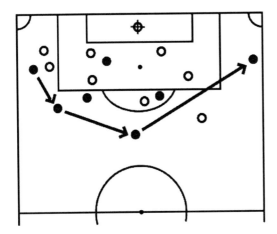

The defence is organised in preparation for an attack from the left winger who is in a very threatening position. The left winger opts to rotate the ball to the right winger. The defence must now reorganise themselves quickly to stop the new threat.

In his game against Mannheimer, Nimzowitch uses a similar technique to win the game.

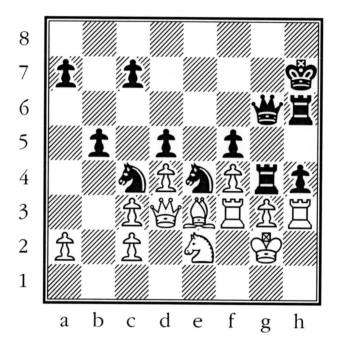

Mannheimer vs Nimzowitch (1930)

Black slowly builds a powerful attack down White's right flank. White has managed to stave it off with a solid but cramped defence. Black can see the lack of mobility in the White defence and quickly switches his attack to the other side, moving his Queen to a6. He then takes the undefended pawn on a2 and brings his own pawn down the open a-file. White is too slow to defend this attack and resigns at this point:

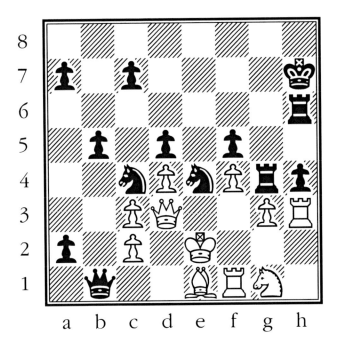

Attacking from the Back

'The King is a fighting piece, use it'
Steinitz

Ajax have traditionally been famous for their attacking style of football. Everything is geared towards attack, and this often includes the goalkeeper. Cruyff used to ask the goalkeeper to act as a sweeper for much of the time so that the team effectively had an extra player.

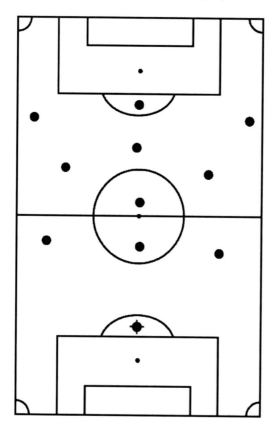

The goalkeeper is available as an eleventh outfield player in Ajax' system.

Towards the end of a chess match is it similarly important to try to attack from the back. This means mobilising the King. The King can be a very effective attacking piece if used correctly and could count as an extra piece in the vital closing stages. Of course, there is a large element of risk in doing this – you have to time it right. However, advocates of attacking chess are all in favour of it.

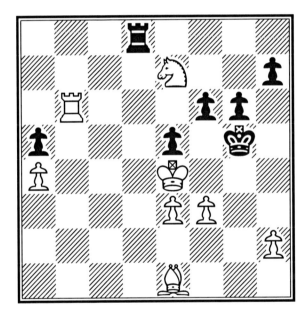

Kasparov vs Rodriguez (1982)

Both Kings are caught up in the main battle ground area.

One of the strategic decisions a coach has to make in football is how far to push up the back line. A high back line has the effect of compressing the overall playing space, making it more difficult for attacks to begin. This gives the defensive players more attacking clout because they are higher up the pitch.

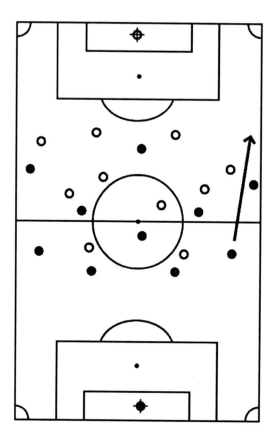

Both teams have pushed up their back lines. With the playing space so compressed, the right back is closer to his attacking team-mates and can interact with the attack more easily. In modern football, games are often so compressed that midfield players do not have enough time or space to be creative. For this reason, defenders are now expected to have attacking abilities, as they will often be the ones with the most time and space.

Chess games where movement and activity are highly constricted in the middle of the board are called 'closed' games. In the 2006 Champions League semi-final (first leg) between Arsenal and Villareal, Villarreal made it a 'closed' game by congesting the midfield. Arsenal were forced to attack down the wings and frequently mobilised their defensive players.

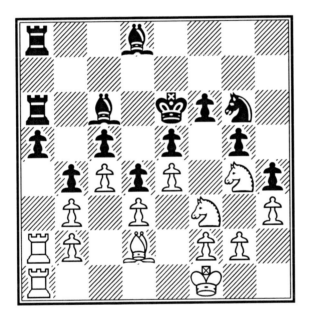

Mok Tze Meng vs Viktor Korchnoi (2004)

This extremely closed game followed the same course as the Arsenal vs Villarreal game.

The Black defense is pushed high and the middle is extremely congested. Black won by creating an opening down White's left wing.

THE SPARE MAN

If a game is very tight and congested it is often difficult to know how to develop your play. A house of cards situation can develop where neither team wants to upset the balance in case it gives a breakthrough to the opposition. In such cases, players will often look for the 'spare' man or piece – the one that is doing least and not so caught up in the deadlock. If no such piece is available, players will try to arrange things so that one piece is freed. The first player to find a spare piece will have the advantage.

In football it is almost impossible for the whole team to be marked out of the game at the same time, so there is usually someone who is spare. The team has to try to find this player and the player himself must be aware of his position. A good example of a player taking up the role was Sol Campbell for Arsenal against Portsmouth.

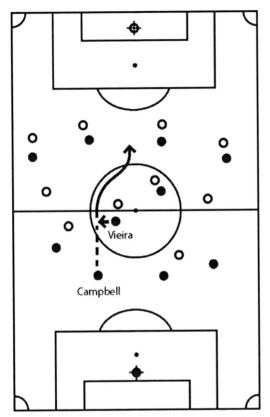

Viera had the ball in midfield but Arsenal were tightly marked all over the field. Campbell was spare at the back so he made a forward run, took up the ball from Viera, and scored.

The following game is very tight and carefully balanced with each piece keeping the structure strong.

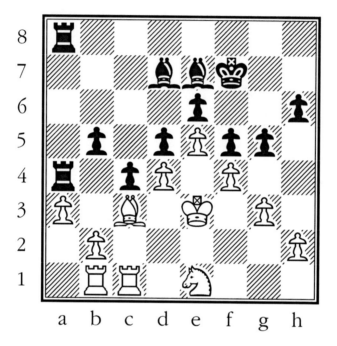

Janowski vs Capablanca (1916)

Capablanca decides to activate the piece that he feels could be doing more and moves the Rook to g8. This proves to be the crucial turning point as the Rook supports a breakthrough on the g-file leading to White's decline.

THE HOLE

Arsenal's run of 49 unbeaten games in the Premiership was achieved partly through having a solid defence but mainly through its consistently brilliant attacking, developed by Arsene Wenger. A particularly effective element of Arsenal's attack during that period was Dennis Bergkamp. A large number of Arsenal's goals came via combinations that involved Bergkamp dropping into the 'hole' between the midfield and attack. In this capacity he proved a devastating connective link in Arsenal's attacking combinations.

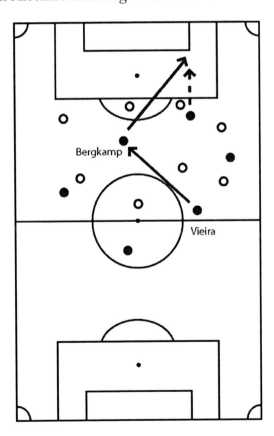

Vieira plays the ball (previous page) through to Bergkamp who is difficult to pick up because he is sitting in the gap between the midfield and defensive lines of four. Bergkamp is then perfectly placed to play a pass through to an attacker.

If a piece can perform a similar role in a chess game, where the defensive pieces are not in a position to put pressure on it, it can wreak havoc.

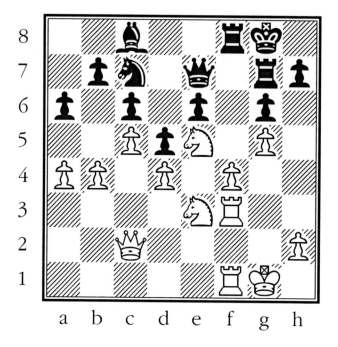

Schlecter vs John (1905)

White managed to station his Knight on e5 for a long period of the game. Black is not in a position to put any pressure on this piece. The Knight became the centre of all White's attacking play and Black eventually folded under the pressure.

Holes are ideal for use as 'outposts' or 'stations'.

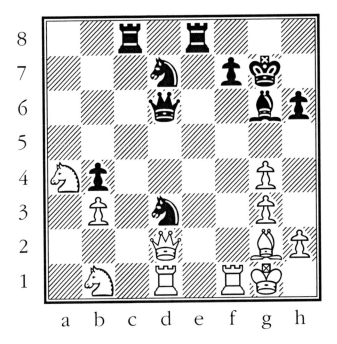

Karpov vs Kasparov (1985)

Black's Knight sat untouchable on the d3 square for a large proportion of the game, acting as an 'outpost' which the other pieces could build off.

A common tactic in football is to station a 'target man' in the hole who the rest of the team can build off. Liverpool use Peter Crouch in a similar way, acting as an 'outpost' to take pressure off Liverpool as they try to work their way out of defence:

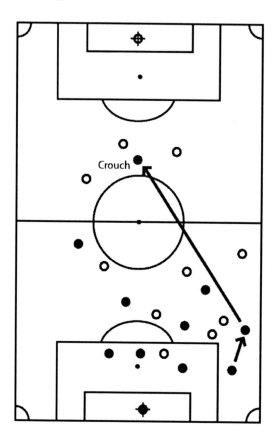

USING THE WIDTH

In the heat of the battle to gain control of the centre it is easy to commit too many pieces to the central area. This can lead to problems on the wings, both in terms of defence and attack. The centre has to be controlled through skill and not just through superior numbers although this hasn't stopped many football teams from adopting the 5-3-2 system.

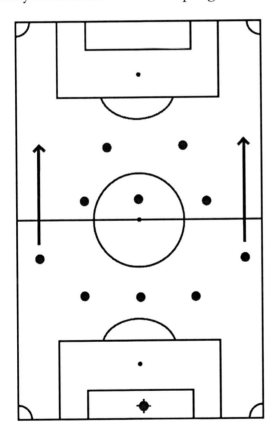

Although the three players in the midfield help the team control the centre, the formation has a significant weakness in that it fails to use the width of the field to the best advantage.

The wing-backs have too much work to do and cannot cover enough ground down the wings to make flank attacks very penetrating.

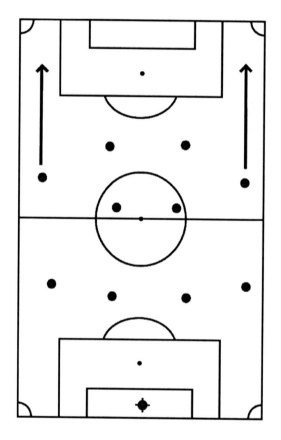

A 4-4-2 formation, on the other hand, makes it more difficult to control the centre, but offers more attacking penetration down the flanks as the wingers are in more advanced positions when they receive the ball.

On the defensive side, teams sometimes commit too many players to the midfield in order to suffocate the opposition, and then get caught out on the wings.

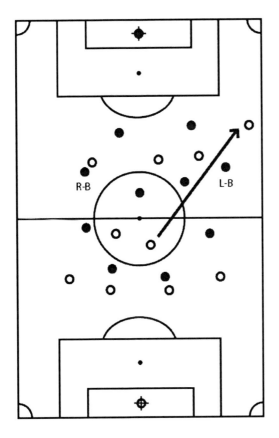

Fulham vs Portsmouth (2005)

The Fulham full-backs move infield to help win the battle for the centre. Portsmouth exploit the space they leave behind them.

Chelsea, under Mourinho, encourage the opposition to crowd the middle of the field so that when the wingers get the ball they have a lot of space to attack.

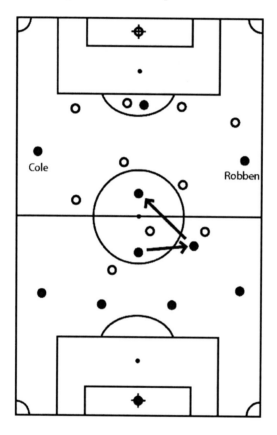

The good connections between the tight three-man midfield encourage the opposition to pressurise that area. The ball can then be released to Robben or Cole who have a lot of attacking space down the flanks.

A similar strategy was used by Steinitz in his game against Chigorin:

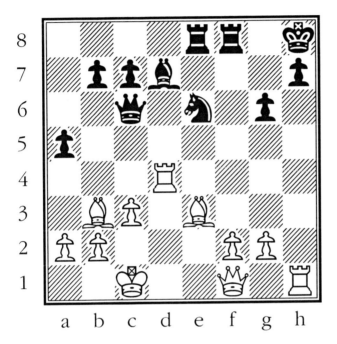

Steinitz vs Chigorin (1892)

Chigorin takes the White Rook in the centre with his Knight, whilst other pieces support the centre from behind. However, this leaves a weakness on Black's left wing and Steinitz exploits this by taking the pawn on h7 with his Rook. The King takes the Rook but then Steinitz begins an attack on the King:

Check! The King moves to g7 but the White Bishop moves to h6 for check again. What follows is a series of checks before Black resigns, knowing his position is too weak.

PART 2 - THE COACH AS CHESS PLAYER

BENITEZ VS ANCELOTTI

Liverpool 3-3 AC Milan, Champions League Final 2006

'At Valencia, sometimes you thought the team moved in such harmony that they were being controlled by him [Benitez] on the touchline.'
Paco Lloret, biographer of Benitez.

The team Rafael Benitez inherited from Gerard Houllier was, in the judgement of Liverpool FC, a failing team. After lacklustre performances, underachievement in all competitions, and mis-spent money, the Liverpool board finally ran out of patience with the French manager. The subsequent search for a new manager ended with the appointment of Rafael Benitez, a Spaniard who had made a name for himself coaching Valencia in the previous three seasons. With limited financial resources, Benitez had created a formidable team which managed to win the Spanish league title twice in three years, beating off competition from the two giants of Spanish football, Barcelona and Real Madrid. During that time Valencia crossed paths with Liverpool in the Champions League. The first game was an embarrassment for Liverpool who, despite fielding a multi-million pound team, looked completely out of their depth. The Valencia players swarmed round their opponents, dazzling them with complex interplay and slicing open their defence time and again. By the end, Liverpool knew they were lucky to escape with a 2-0 defeat. For the return match, Liverpool brushed themselves down, rallied together and came out fighting in front of their home fans. However, this fighting spirit once again had little effect on Valencia who easily controlled the game again, and came away with a comfortable 1-0 victory.

Two years later, the Liverpool players had still not forgotten the experience. When the Liverpool chief executive, Rick Parry, asked the players to name the best team they had played against in the previous few years, they all agreed that it was Valencia, despite having faced many of the top teams in Europe. This confirmed in Parry's mind that Benitez was the best coach available. Valencia were not a team full of star players, but they had consistently performed at an exceptional level, and it was clear to many people that the main factor behind this was the quality of their coach.

The expectations facing Benitez when he accepted the job at Liverpool were extraordinarily high – perhaps unrealistically high. These expectations were founded on Liverpool's desperate desire to recreate their immensely successful past. His task was to close the large gap in quality between Liverpool and the top teams in the English league without spending as much money. Under normal circumstances, this would seem unreasonable, but since Benitez had done a similar thing at Valencia, the situation was different. A year later, the decision to appoint Benitez had proved to be inspired. After Benitez left, Valencia immediately slumped, dropping from first to seventh in the end of season table. Liverpool, on the other hand, began a gradual rise which culminated in securing the Champions League title in May 2005.

It is widely believed that Rafael Benitez's tactics were the main factor behind Liverpool's highly unexpected success in Europe's most elite competition. A team that lacked the quality of many other teams involved somehow managed to win it. This was because they were steered with the tactical acumen of a Grandmaster by their chess-playing manager. The fact that Liverpool had made it through to the Final in the first place was something of a miracle. After all, Benitez had had neither the time nor the funds to replace the vast majority of the players that Houllier had been working with. Despite this, he had managed to mastermind victories over

Juventus and Chelsea, the respective leaders of the Italian and English leagues, en-route to the Final. He did this primarily by organising the defence so well that it was very difficult to score against them. This led to criticisms that Liverpool were negative and boring, and many claimed they didn't merit a place in the final of the most prestigious club competition in the world, seeing the pairing against Milan as a woeful mis-match. However, the extraordinary game that followed silenced all this criticism.

Ancelotti's plan for the first half worked perfectly. An early goal made things difficult for Liverpool but the reason they went 3-0 down before half-time was mainly a result of Milan's exploitation of weaknesses.

Milan identified Traore as the weakest defender on the ball. Therefore all efforts were made to apply pressure when Finnan had possession on the right so that Liverpool were forced to rotate the ball to Traore on the left. Liverpool were then unable to develop any fluid attacks because even at this early point they had stagnated. Traore did not have the attacking abilities to create anything of any value and so Milan were happy to let him have the ball while they marked all the other players.

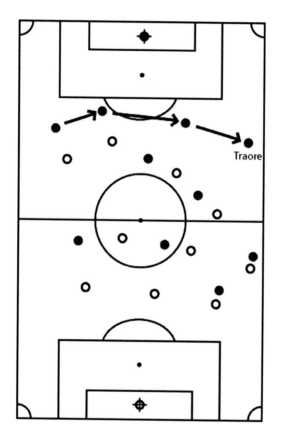

In this way, Milan's overall defensive setup was largely active rather than just reactive - a technique discussed in the chapter 'Pressing'. By shutting off certain channels, they dictated how Liverpool built their attacks.

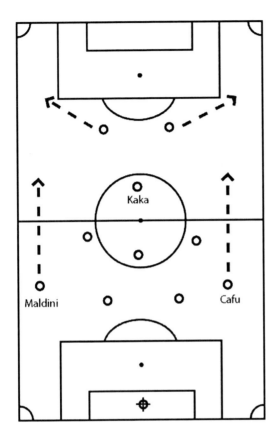

Milan's general formation was 4-3-1-2. This differs from the standard 4-4-2 formation in that the attacking emphasis is not so focused down the wings. Instead they crammed the midfield, with Kaka placed between the midfield and attack to provide a potent threat through the centre. The width they did have was provided by their full-backs, Cafu and Maldini, and by their strikers who compensated for the lack of wingers by drifting wide.

As Liverpool's general formation was 4-4-2, their strategic plan was to create attacking pressure down the wings. It became a question of whether Liverpool's width or Milan's pressure through the centre would prevail. This was a strategically similar situation to the Botvinnik – Capablanca game discussed in the chapter 'Build-up Play'.

Unfortunately for Liverpool, Milan's passing connections were superior. These strong connections enabled them to dominate the midfield and maintain flowing supply lines to Kaka, allowing him to inflict a huge amount of damage. It is therefore no surprise that Milan's goals to make it 2-0 and 3-0 came through the centre rather than from the wings. The goals were very similar and somewhat inevitable because the same situation was happening over and over again. Benitez's conundrum at the start of the game was whether to give special attention to Kaka by adding an extra defensive player, or to try to take the initiative with a more attacking formation. In the end he decided the latter option was more likely to cause difficulties for Milan. Thus the central midfielders, Alonso and Gerrard, on top of being given the task of trying to start off attacks, had to keep a defensive eye on Kaka all the time.

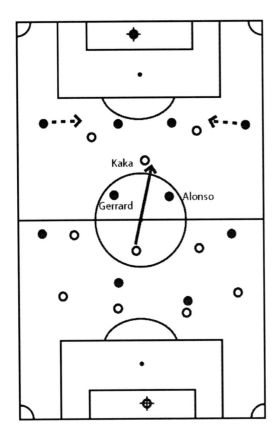

Unfortunately for Benitez they were caught between both roles for most of the first half, neither stopping Kaka nor starting any attacking moves. Several times Kaka broke free without being picked up. Each time this happened the Liverpool full backs would move infield because Milan did not offer any attacking threat down the wings.

At half-time Liverpool seemed a write-off. Many had predicted that Milan would win the game easily, and they appeared to be correct. Liverpool hadn't even played particularly badly, they just seemed to be out of their depth. Accordingly, the bookmakers put the price of a Liverpool win at a staggering 100-1.

Benitez's masterstroke at half-time was to substitute Finnan for Hamann. This left only 3 defenders and - rather alarmingly for Liverpool - left Traore, the weakest Liverpool defender in the first half, in a more important central defensive role. However, rather than crumbling, the defence actually became stronger and tighter.

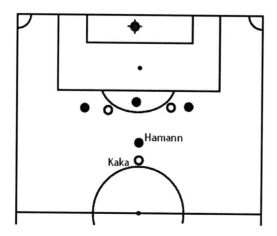

Hamann filled the gap that Kaka had exploited to great effect in the first-half, causing the connective supply line to the Milan strikers to be cut out. This meant that the loss of a defender didn't matter so much, especially since Milan weren't attacking from the wings. By sacrificing a defender in this way, Benitez was adhering to Steinitz's principle of economic defence.

The main effect of bringing on Hamann was that Liverpool won back the midfield. This was not just a question of extra numbers. As in chess, it is *how* the players interact in the middle that determines whether you win the midfield. The coach, like the chess player, must use his players so that their strengths are being used to the fullest. Another set of players may not have responded as well as these players did. It is not just a question of putting players in the correct positions, but putting the right players in the correct positions. Crucially, having been suffocated in the first half, Gerrard and Alonso could breathe again and began expressing themselves because Gerrard was now playing ahead of Alonso. Liverpool became far more fluid in midfield and offered a new attacking threat in the form of Gerrard. Ultimately, it was through this new threat that Liverpool worked their way back into the game. Instead of the striker Baros being alone when the ball came in from the wings, he was supported by Gerrard and Garcia. At the same time these players were higher up when Milan had the ball and so they pressured Milan higher up the field.

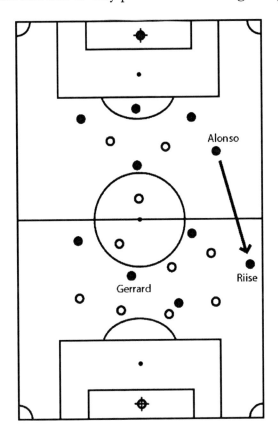

Now, instead of Traore constantly ending up with the ball, it would increasingly be the more creative Alonso who would have space in deep positions to pick out a good pass. Furthermore, Riise was able to move further up the field to receive the ball on the left wing as the Milan defence were committing more bodies to midfield positions to deal with the new Liverpool threat in midfield. Meanwhile, when Carragher - one of the centre-backs - was left unpressured, he would come roaming forward rather than holding back. Now that Liverpool had the initiative at last, he had to make use of it by attacking more.

Milan were unable to cope with this total and sudden change in the dynamic of the game and conceded three goals in eight minutes, to take the game into extra time.

With the matched tied at 3-3 after 120 minutes, Liverpool went on to win the game, dramatically and famously, on penalties.

.

PART 3 - GENERAL STRATEGIC CONCEPTS FOR CONTROLLING THE GAME

THE INITIATIVE

The initiative is a term used to describe the ability of a football team or chess player to make threats towards the opponent. The team or player who holds the initiative can be said to have the most attacking potential at that point. The degree to which players value the initiative varies according to how they like to build attacks. Players who prefer to counter-attack are often willing to let the opposition have the initiative for much of the game. One such example is GM Korchnoi who says, 'I do not like to attack first... I prefer to give my opponent the opportunity to attack'.

A large factor in determining who holds the initiative in a football game is 'home advantage'. Results prove that there is a significant advantage to playing at home. It is rare for a team to win more games away from home over the course of a season. Familiarity with the stadium, coupled with vocal support, gives teams the confidence and the energy to seize the initiative for long spells of the game. The difference between playing at home and playing away in football can be likened to the difference between playing with White and Black in chess. A lot of it is psychological, as in football, but there is a definite advantage to having the first move because you are essentially a move up and therefore able to dictate the play from an early point. Often in tournaments the chess masters aim to win their games with White and draw with Black. In the group stages of the Champions League, teams think the same way. They are happy to play for a draw in their away games in the belief that they will collect enough points in their home games to take them through.

With or without an advantage, one must work hard to gain the initiative. One way to secure it is to play at a high tempo, making it difficult for the opposition to keep up. 'Tempo' describes the directness of a move in terms of its attacking threat. For instance, if from a given point you checkmate an opponent in three moves, you are playing at a higher tempo than if you checkmate them in ten moves. Both games can be exhilarating when played at a high tempo, but it is very difficult to maintain as you can lose control over what you are doing easily. The nature of the games is such that playing at any one tempo does not tend to produce the best results. In the majority of cases it is important to have variety by mixing fast, aggressive moves with slower, less immediately destructive ones.

The Latvian Grandmaster Mikhail Tal took chess into a new realm of inventiveness by throwing out the old doctrines of controlled positional play and unleashing a new style of high tempo, daring, complicated chess which dazzled the chess world and won many admirers. His philosophy was to maintain the initiative throughout the entire game. As long as the game was played at a high tempo he was confident his opponent would not be able to handle the intensity. This is indeed what happened in many of his games. Opponents would fail to remain composed enough to exploit any of his weaknesses.

A similar tactical development took place in football in the 1970s when Ajax developed the new philosophy of 'Total Football'. This was similar to Tal's approach to chess in that it was designed to lift the game out of the tactical rigidity of the times, and, like Tal, they achieved this through elevating the complexity of the game and giving a new license to unrestrained attacking. Defenders could pour forward into attack as they wished and other players would have the presence of mind to cover for them. As a result, it was difficult for the opposition to know what to expect or how to counter-attack and ultimately Ajax won three European Cups in a row.

Renus Michels, credited as the inventor of Total Football, said of this method, '"Total Football" and its attacking pressure are very spectacular. It places great demands on individual and team tactical excellence... An absolute prerequisite, to master such a team tactical aspect, is that all the players possess a positive mentality'. Tal likewise could only play such tactics with an extremely positive mentality because it was so dangerous. Only total belief in his ability to retain the initiative could allow him to commit so much to attack. There is a fine line between brilliance and recklessness.

Michels knew only too well the importance of retaining the initiative, just as Tal did: 'You always take the initiative… you must do that. However, if you fail to carry the play and get under pressure, then the opponent will take advantage of the weak aspects of the style you are playing'. GM Spassky points out a similar thing in Tal's style: 'He played best, of course, when he held the initiative. Without it he would suffocate'. The main weak aspect that Michels refers to is the large amount of space that is left behind the defence. This required both Ajax and Tal to be extremely resourceful in defence.

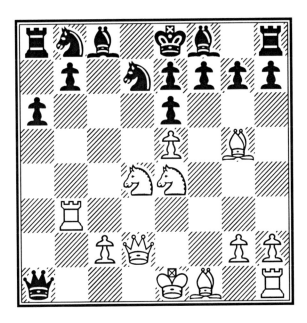

Tal vs Tolush (1956)

At first glance, Tal's position here looks almost amateur in its recklessness. The Black Queen has torn into his pieces and now threatens the King even at this early stage in the game. However, Tal has calculated that his defence can cope, despite the precarious position, and his attacking pieces go on to win the game for him.

Jeremy Silman splits chess 'initiative' into two types. The first involves a 'dynamic advantage'. In this situation the player must play at a high tempo to capitalise on an advantage he has gained. Counter-attacking teams, who are prepared to surrender the initiative for most of the game, thrive off 'dynamic advantages', hoping to score goals in the sporadic, temporary moments which offer them attacking opportunities. As Jeremy Silman explains, 'a dynamic advantage centers around temporary items' and will 'often dissipate with the passage of time'. Exceptional attacking players like Tal and Kasparov could sustain a 'dynamic advantage' for almost entire games, but this is rare.

Of course, a high tempo does not in itself secure the initiative. In chess, if you have no 'dynamic advantage' inherent in your position, you should not try to force a high tempo with direct, attacking moves. You have to make a judgement about whether a 'dynamic advantage' actually exists. The Argentinian World Cup team of 2006 were excellent at determining when they had a 'dynamic advantage'. Only at such a point would they raise the tempo of their game.

A 'static' advantage is more long-term. It is something that will provide a springboard for attacks later in the game. This comes down to better positioning and connections, where the pieces or players are working more harmoniously. Having a static advantage allows you to control the game and wait for the right moment to convert this into an attack. When Argentina had no 'dynamic advantage' they would play at a slower tempo, but still retain the initiative through good passing and movement. Thus, through varying the tempo over the course of a game, they could retain the initiative throughout.

English football, on the other hand, has often been criticised for its penchant for playing football at a tempo which is too fast for its own good. After a series of embarrassing defeats for English teams in the European competitions throughout the 1990s, there followed a period of introspection where many pundits and coaches decided that the continental style of slower more controlled football was leaving the English behind. However, since the introduction of Arsene Wenger and a handful of other foreign coaches into the Premiership, English football has been able to absorb many elements of European football whilst preserving its own high tempo game. Indeed, the transformation has been so dramatic that nowadays one could pose the opposite argument: that English club football leads the way in Europe. In consecutive years the Serie A leaders Juventus were knocked out of the Champions League by British teams 30 points off the top of the Premiership table. One major reason seemed to be that Juventus were unable to adapt to the tempo that Liverpool and Arsenal played at. Here were English teams playing at a ferociously fast tempo but now in a more controlled way.

Despite this, the England national team have continued to have problems with tempo.

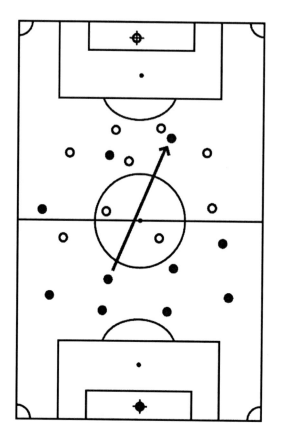

England vs Paraguay (2006)

Teams must judge the right time to make a quiet, 'slow' move, and when to make an aggressive attacking move. In the second half of the World Cup game against Paraguay the England midfielders continued to make fast, attacking passes up the field where other teams would have chosen to slow the tempo down. The strikers were isolated as the other players were not well enough developed to offer support, meaning England lost the ball regularly. A simpler pass, designed to facilitate a more gradual build up, would have been preferable on many occasions.

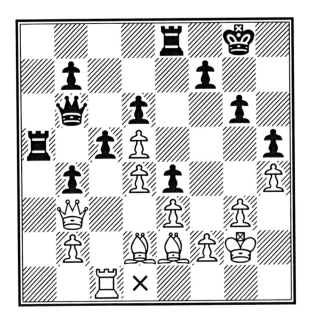

Bareev vs Volkov (2005)

White moves his Rook to X, demonstrating, unlike England in the last example, that he understands the value of a 'slow', understated move in aiding the overall development of the play.

Another way of gaining the initiative is through **controlling space**. Nowadays, when football statisticians show possession statistics they often take into account the territory that teams have kept possession of the ball in.

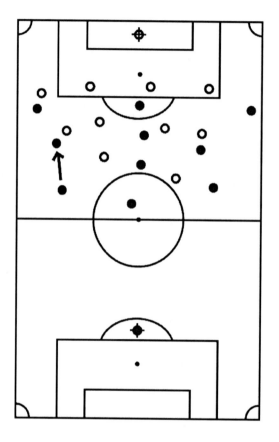

Ajax (1994/1995)

Ajax, under Louis Van Gaal, would pin the opposition back until they were controlling ¾ of the pitch. They often maintained this for long spells of their games, whilst waiting patiently for the correct moment to break down the defence. They were so confident in their ability to keep possession of the ball that they were prepared to risk leaving a huge amount of space behind their defence.

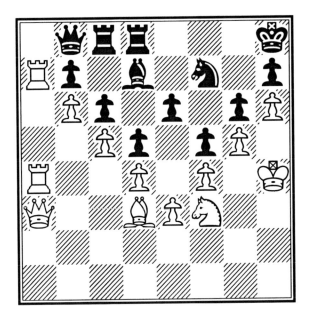

Capablanca vs Treybal (1929)

There can be few examples which demonstrate one side controlling the board space so thoroughly as White in this game. Like Ajax in the previous example, Capablanca has total control of the space, and now just has to wait for the right moment to open up the defence.

It is a valuable skill to be able to judge the subtle changes in initiative that occur over the course of a game. There are lots of clichés, which seem annoyingly obvious, about the best teams in football taking their chances when they come. However, the serious point is that the top teams know how to capitalise on the 'ebb and flow' of a game. In some games, the match will be so one sided that there will hardly be any flux in initiative. In most games, however, each side will have periods during which the attacking momentum is with them. The important thing is to concentrate on weathering the storm when the momentum is against you, and to move in for the kill when it is with you. If you try to disturb this ebb and flow you will get into trouble. As Steinitz said, 'only the player with the initiative has the right to attack'.

THE MINI-BATTLES

Chess players engage in many small battles during a game which will eventually effect the overall game. For instance, a player may have in mind five mini-battles that he wants to win. He may want to occupy a certain square, drive back a piece, prevent the opponent from moving on to a particular square, dominate a file etc. He hopes that by doing this things will fall into place and opportunities will arrive, even if he doesn't know exactly how yet.

In football, many teams approach the game in a similar way. Two players may battle for domination of a certain area; a player might want to mark another out of the game; a target man and a defender will struggle for aerial domination. If a team can win these small battles, it will often win the game.

However, approaching the games in such a way can be limiting. Simpler teams will have these mini-battles in mind but will often have no clear ideas about how they are going to create a good goalscoring chance. More sophisticated teams, like Arsenal, are thinking about the overall design of their play all the time. They know what to expect from each other in terms of the movement, passing and positioning and will have a clearer idea about how they are going to score, even from the early stages of the build-up. They may confidently ignore the kind of maxims that simpler teams will stick to: they may play it into tight areas rather than playing an obvious ball into space; when a winger has the ball he won't necessarily cross it, as other teams would; a player with a shooting chance may still pass it.

Similarly, top-level chess players may happily ignore the kind of maxims that lesser players will stick to, as these may conflict with their long-term plan. Seemingly good opportunities may be ignored whilst moves which would seem reckless to a weaker player may actually be pulled off.

BALANCE

*'One of the toughest team tactical assignments for the coach is
to keep the tactical balance in the team'*
Rinus Michels

One of the beautiful things about chess and football is the
way they are balanced in terms of the importance of attack
and defence. Despite tactical innovations and theories of all
kinds that have developed over many years, it has still not been
proven that it is better to play offensively or defensively.

In the Champions League 2005, the teams that made it
through to the Quarter-Finals were generally defensively
minded, which perhaps left some fundamental doubts in the
minds of those coaches who preferred dynamic attacking
football. It also helped the argument of those who suggest that
the modern game has swung out of balance and become too
defensive. Arsène Wenger was called naïve for continuing to
play the attacking game he believed in so strongly, as Arsenal
crashed out in the Round of 16. Despite all this, Wenger stayed
true to his philosophy the next year, and his team managed
to reach the Final where they met perhaps the most attack-
orientated team in Europe, Barcelona.

The chess world has also seen a healthy balance between
defence and attack. The World Championship has been won
not only by ultra-attacking players like Tal, Alekhine and
Kasparov but also by cautious, defensive players like Petrosian,
Steinitz, and Lasker.

The balance between attack and defence is the most crucial
balance to find in chess and football. Often in chess you may
think you are winning – your pawns are dominating the centre,
the opponent shows no signs of attacking in any way, and your
pieces are spaced nicely to begin attacks in different channels
and on different sides of the board. However, a little later your
whole position seems to have crumbled. Your pieces seem like

they are too far forward and there is space behind the pawns for the opponent to exploit. You find that you cannot get your pieces back in time to defend. Essentially, this is what often happens in football both in the short term and over a whole game. The game changes and unless you have a good balance of attack and defense you won't be able to adapt. If you upset the balance you are asking for trouble.

Rafael Benitez talks regularly about the need to find the correct balance between attack and defence. It is difficult to achieve because balance is based on a number of variables which change over the course of a season or indeed a single game. Factors that influence the emphasis a team should place on attack or defence include, a) their own confidence in attack and defense respectively, b) whether they are playing at home or away, c) the attacking and defensive qualities of the opposition, d) the need to draw, win or achieve a win by a particular margin, e) the type of football that suits the players in the team. If Liverpool are playing a team at the bottom of the league table, they are more likely to put a little more emphasis on attacking than defending. Likewise, if they are playing a top quality European team, they might concentrate more on defending.

We tend to categorise footballers into attackers, midfielders and defenders. However, this should not cloud the fact that each player on the pitch is both an attacking and a defensive entity. When the opposition 'defenders' have the ball you expect your 'attackers' to put pressure on them. Thus the attackers are at this point fulfilling a defensive duty. Similarly, attacks are normally built up from 'defence', making the defenders part of the overall attack. In chess, the situation is the same. The optimal state is for the pieces to be serving attacking and defensive functions simultaneously.

Balance is a difficult thing to achieve and can be upset by philosophies which are too rigid. A notable example is the Italian national team who underachieved in the 2002 World Cup and 2004 European Championship because they placed too much emphasis on defence.

PART 4 - PSYCHOLOGICAL FACTORS

AWARENESS

'Every player has to understand the whole geometry of the whole pitch'
Gerard Van Der Lem

There are many types of awareness required to play football well. Awareness of space is of primary importance. On top of this, a player must always be alert to the positions and movements of his team-mates and the opponents. The best players are only able to make good decisions by being aware of the whole situation on the pitch. Such awareness reduces the chance of overlooking possibilities and is vital for keeping the overall shape of a team. It also means they can pick out the best option quickly without having to spend too much time looking around. Keeping aware of the positions and movements of 22 players at the same time is not easy and requires years of practice.

In chess you must also think quickly and broadly, taking in everything that is happening across the whole board. The faster a player can take in the whole situation, the faster he can focus his attention on one particular area. Grandmasters can instinctively pick out which areas to focus on. As in football, this ability develops the more you play. You begin to get a 'sense' of your pieces and the potentials on the board, just as footballers develop a sense of where their team-mates will be and what they are going to do.

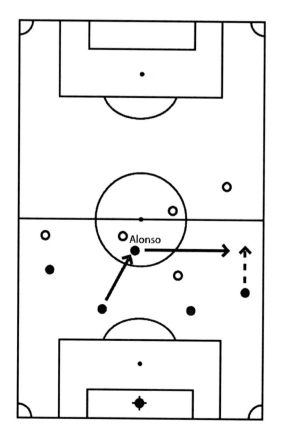

Xabi Alonso's position of defensive midfielder requires a high level of awareness of the whole field. Often heavily pressured when he receives the ball, he has to choose a pass immediately. This requires him to quickly decide which players are in the best position to receive a pass, which players are under too much pressure and should be overlooked, and whether it would be safer to return the ball to the goalkeeper. Since he often has his back to the attacking players on his team when he receives the ball, he must turn quickly and assess the options at great speed if he wants to make a pass forward.

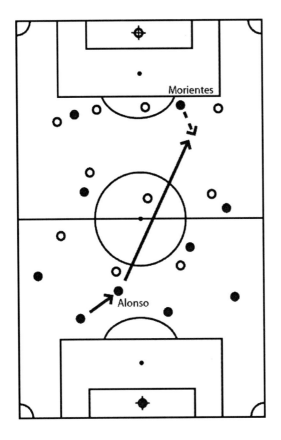

In this situation Alonso receives the ball, turns, assesses the situation of his team-mates, notices that there is a gap between the opposition's midfield and defence, and picks out Morientes as the best option.

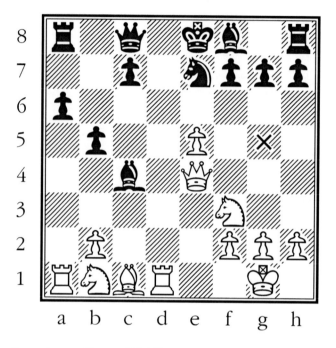

Smyslov vs Euwe (1948)

How quickly can you take in everything that is happening on the board? The experienced chess player will immediately notice a number of important things: the direct threats (e.g. a1 Rook against the pawn on a6, the Queen on the Rook at a8); the space that the pieces are covering (e.g the White Rook covering the whole d file); the potential connective points between pieces (e.g the g5 square for White, where Bishop and Knight can meet); the weak spots of both sides (e.g the uncastled King on the e8 square).

CREATIVITY

'The idea comes before the logical argument'
Gerald Abrahams

It is one thing to be able to calculate complex tactical combinations, but before this we have to have an idea of what we want to achieve in the first place. All football teams like to have at least one player who has enough creativity to do the unexpected. Often this player is able to do this because he has superior technical skill. However, it is also about having the liveliness of mind to come up with a solution that others may not have seen. As Eric Cantona says,

> 'You cannot be a great player without being intelligent. You need to be very quick to read the runs of team-mates. In one second, you have to imagine a lot of possibilities and decide immediately. It's like geometry in your head. Sometimes, there are 60,000 people in the stand and you give a good ball to somebody to score and nobody could see the ball.'

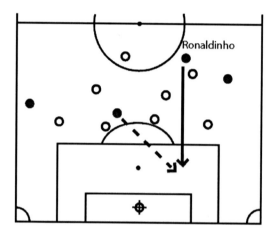

AC Milan vs Barcelona (2006)

With 'geometry in his head', Ronaldinho picks out Guily with a pass nobody saw coming to create the only goal in a 1-0 win over AC Milan.

It is often surprising what you can do on a chess board if you stop thinking in the normal logical way. For instance, it is sometimes useful to employ a method of reverse thinking where you decide what you would like to happen and see if you can find a way of achieving it. This is often the best way to find devastating combinations.

Alternatively, it is sometimes worth jumping into the unknown in chess and seeing what happens. Even at tournament level Mikhail Tal would often throw himself into situations which he wasn't sure he could get out of. If the main road was blocked he would take the unfamiliar back streets because he trusted his deeper sense of where he was going.

DARING

'Intelligence without audaciousness is not enough'
Garry Kasparov

Creative ideas are only useful if they can be converted into reality. This requires confidence and daring. In football, confidence must be a collective thing. Players must be prepared to do something dangerous and trust that their team-mates will be alert to it. Such collective trust can greatly improve the harmony of a team. Even the most simple passing and movement requires a lot of trust. You cannot just pass directly to other players and hope to keep the ball; you must pass into space, trusting yourself to weight the pass properly and trusting another player to meet it. As the former England national coach Sven Goran Eriksson says, 'the ability to make the right decision - and then dare to do the right thing in all situations - is decisive at the top of the modern game.'

Chess also requires daring because making the easy move will not allow you to control the board. If you want to win the battle for the centre at the beginning you must play carefully but **aggressively**. If you are too timid and cautious you will lose ground.

This is a typical opening situation which seems evenly balanced.

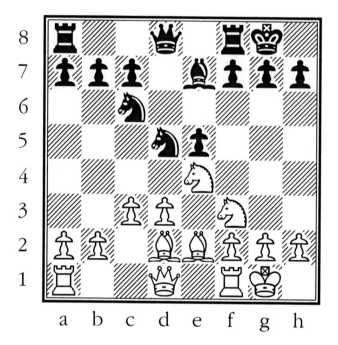

Black sees an opportunity to put White on the back foot early by moving his pawns to f5 and then g5. This drives back the White Knights and gives Black an opportunity to bring his Knight forward:

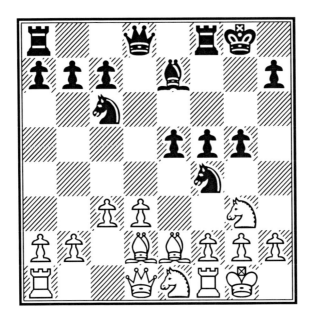

This is a great example of what Erikkson calls 'daring to do the right thing'. Many players may have seen the potential here, but how many would have had the audacity to leave the King unprotected like this so early in the game? Black went on to win quickly with a direct attack on the White King.

CONCENTRATION

'One bad move nullifies forty good ones'
Horowitz

Chess is the most intellectually demanding sport there is, and it therefore goes without saying that concentration is very important. It is easy to be lazy and fail to think things through rigorously, especially if you are in a winning position, but concentration must be kept up right until the end, otherwise you can easily lose any lead you have gained. As GM Lasker said, 'The hardest game to win is the won game'. It is notoriously easy to make major blunders in chess, and one blunder can cost you the game. There are many instances where grandmasters have thrown away good positions they should have won from, and some have made errors that even beginners wouldn't make.

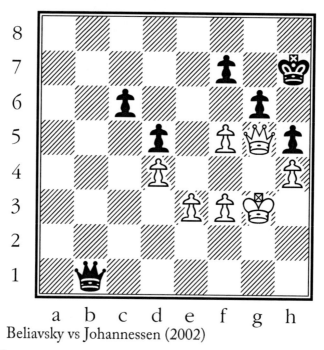

Beliavsky vs Johannessen (2002)

In an evenly poised game Beliavsky makes the worst possible move by moving his king to f4 (previous page). Johannessen moves his Queen to b8 and it's checkmate!

In football blunders are also common, and they are normally caused by a slip of concentration.

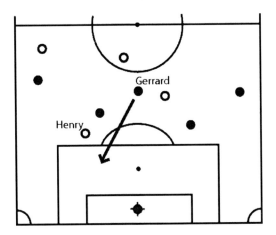

England vs France (2004)

After a well played 90 minutes England seemed to have secured a 1-1 draw with France until one slip of concentration by Steven Gerrard, who played the ball straight into the path of Henry, gifted France a victory.

Stereotypical views that see chess as a purely intellectual game and football as a fundamentally physical game are very limited. Top level football demands mental strength as much as physical strength. Since many games are won 1-0, managers are always stressing the need for their players to concentrate fully for the entire 90 minutes. Ajax Amsterdam take this so seriously that they have built concentration exercises into their youth development programme, believing that mental fitness should be nurtured from an early age. By the same token chess players have to be in good physical condition, otherwise their mental strength will be weakened. The great chess teacher

Bruce Pandolfini explains, 'If your concentration wavers for even a second, you're dead. That kind of mental discipline has a physical component. Sometimes you can win through sheer force of stamina'.

EMOTIONAL CONTROL

'A chessmaster should be a combination of a beast of prey and a monk.'
Capablanca

A player's approach to each game has to be similar from a psychological point of view. As in most sports, there has to be a controlled aggression. It is very easy in chess and football to let emotion dictate your play. Emotion is useful to an extent because it keeps you sharp and determined. However, if you let your emotions control you, your performance will deteriorate rapidly. A team that is losing in a football match must remain calm to get back into the match. They cannot panic and must continue to build up play in a controlled way. In chess, you are wasting your mental energies if you start to get too angry or frustrated. Thus, in both these games there is a premium on emotional control.

In other sports, such as tennis or cricket, if you are playing better than the opposition you are rewarded with regular point accumulations. In chess and football, you can be superior for a long period of time and get no reward. It is natural that frustration will creep in at such points, and this is what the most successful players know how to control. Jose Mourinho cites this as one of the most important requirements for performing optimally. 'Without emotional control you cannot play, influence. You have to be cool.'

By the same token, players must not only be able to control their frustration, but know how to neutralise their enthusiasm when things are going well. The great director Stanley Kubrick sums this up nicely. 'Chess teaches you to control the initial excitement you feel when you see something that looks good and it trains you to think objectively when you're in trouble'.

It is perhaps the large amount of confidence, concentration

and emotional control needed to play either game well that has prompted people to praise them for their character-building qualities. The American president Benjamin Franklin was a huge fan of chess and believed it to have a relevance to life as a whole: 'The game of chess is not merely an idle amusement; several very valuable qualities of the mind are to be acquired and strengthened by it, so as to become habits ready on all occasions; for life is a kind of chess'.

SURPRISE

'A player surprised is half beaten'
Proverb

Part of developing expertise in football or chess involves becoming familiar with a huge bank of situations. Grandmasters can recognise thousands of board situations almost instantly because they have seen them so many times before. Similarly, a footballer who has been playing in a single position for his whole career will have experienced the same situations so many times that he will be able to make decisions very quickly. Whilst this kind of fast mental processing is necessary to play the games at a high level, it can also have the detrimental effect of throwing a player off balance when something unexpected happens. In such a situation a player is thrown into unfamiliar terrain and forced to re-evaluate what he thought he understood. In light of this, surprise can be a useful weapon, especially for weaker players who can potentially exploit the complacency of stronger ones. In football this can take the form of a defender charging up the field with the ball as Sol Campbell did in the 1998 World Cup a number of times. In chess it could be bringing the pawns that should be protecting the King out into the attack. Such moves often succeed because the opposition is thrown by them. By doing such a thing you temporary uproot all their thought processes to gain a slight advantage.

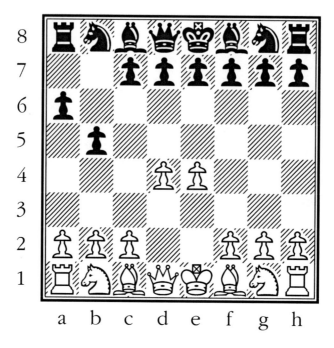

Karpov vs Miles (1980)

Knowing that Karpov had superior knowledge of opening positions Miles decided to play possibly the most unlikely opening ever seen in top level chess, moving his pawns to a6 and b5. Karpov certainly hadn't prepared for what seemed like the moves of an amateur. As a result, Karpov, despite being a far superior player, became very unsettled throughout the game, and lost without much of a fight.

One of the most famous surprise moves of all time was actually made by a computer. The move by Deep Blue which Kasparov calls the 'hand of God' threw Kasparov so much that he lost a game he could have drawn and couldn't regain his composure for any of the following games. Kasparov believed that he could predict the computer's thought processes and felt that it was impossible for the computer to make the move it made.

PART 5 - GENERAL FEATURES AND AESTHETICS

COMEBACKS

Comebacks are one of the things that make sport in general so exciting. They can happen in any sport, but chess and football are almost unique in the speed with which they can occur. In tennis, a player who is two sets down will require a lot of time to claw back. Compare this to football where the whole course of a game can be reversed in just a couple of minutes, as occurred famously in the 1999 Champions League final when Manchester United overturned Bayern Munich's lead to win 2-1 in the dying moments of the game. In chess, whole games can be changed with just one or two moves.

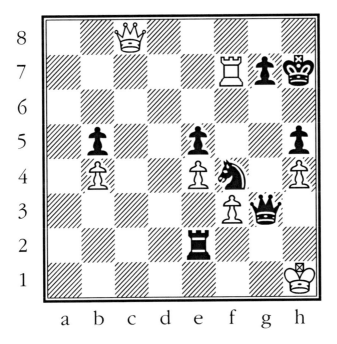

Evans vs Reshevsky (1963)

In one move Black will achieve checkmate with the Queen moving to g2. It seems clear to everybody that White has lost. Despite this, White manages to get a draw by forcing the following:

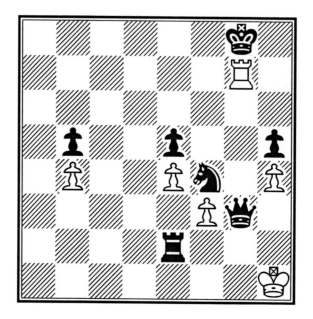

Whatever Black does now, White will be unable to move any piece on his next move. The game is a stalemate.

LUCK

'A good player is always lucky'
Capablanca

Most would agree that luck often plays a significant role in determining the outcome of a football match. Refereeing mistakes, blunders and goals against the run of play can hand teams 'lucky' victories or draws. On the other hand, it is also widely believed that luck does not enter into chess, and indeed this is sometimes cited as one of the attractions of the game. However, this is not true at all. Whilst not having to rely on subjective refereeing decisions, chess nevertheless involves a lot of luck of a different sort.

You can be lucky in the sense that you have played badly but the opponent has missed the opportunity to punish you. It is fair to say that Bronstein was extremely lucky to beat Petrosian in this game:

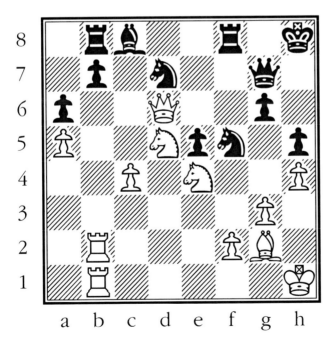

Petrosian vs Bronstein (1956)

After a well played game, Petrosian has Bronstein pinned back and now has plenty of options for attack. However, with his next move he manages to overlook the fact that the Knight on f5 is threatening his Queen, and moves another piece. Bronstein duly takes the Queen and Petrosian resigns.

Another way you can be lucky is by finding yourself in a good position without having consciously set it up. This is something every chess player regularly experiences, but tends to stay quiet about.

As nobody is a perfect chess player, there are always countless elements of every game which are out of our control. We often fail to predict where opponents will move and we overlook many possibilities. Since we are not in complete control, luck inherently plays a large part. As a result, the best player does not always win, just as the best team does not always win in football. We all feel aggrieved when we are victims of this, but at the same time we recognise that the games would be less interesting without these 'injustices'.

STYLE

"Every top player has his own style, just as every painter has his own personal signature". Kramnik

One of the things that people find so enjoyable about football is the way games can be so different from one to the next. This has a great deal to do with the differing styles of play that teams have. The top teams in European football all have their own particular brand of football. Broadly speaking, Italian teams are known for their tight and stubbornly defensive style; Spanish teams for their dazzling interplay; Dutch teams for their controlled build-up play and flexible systems and English teams for their fast, aggressive, open style. It is frequently commented that Italian teams play a 'chess-like' style of football, because their games are so tactical and tight. This totally overlooks the fact that chess games can be wide open, with end to end attacking, just like the most exciting football games. Kasparov, for instance, played a very dynamic, attacking game, often leaving space at the back for opponents to attack. In this respect his approach was similar to that of Barcelona under Frank Rijkaard, who play extremely intricate and complicated attacking football, but leave a lot of space at the back. Like Kasparov, Barcelona have to defend with extreme efficiency, with extra players supporting the defenders at exactly the right time, because they simply commit fewer players to defense than other teams. Whilst most teams play four or even five defenders at the back Barcelona traditionally only have three in their 3-1-3-3 formation. By playing this formation, Rijkaard offers the opposition a lot of encouragement to attack because there is so much room to exploit.

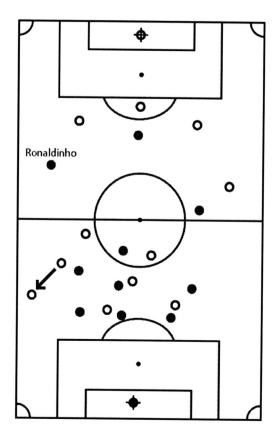

Ronaldinho

Instead of tracking back, Ronaldinho stays up-field when the opposition have the ball. Once Barcelona regain the ball they play it to Ronaldinho who has a lot of room to attack the defenders. This can make the game very stretched.

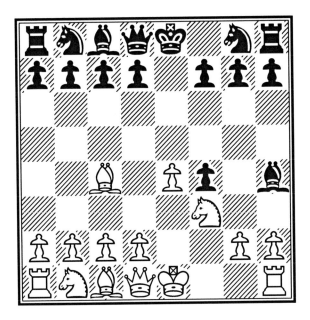

Short vs Kasparov (1993)

With only his fourth move Kasparov has already put Short in check, but leaves his opponent with space to attack the centre. This provokes a game of end to end attacking which ends with both Kings under siege:

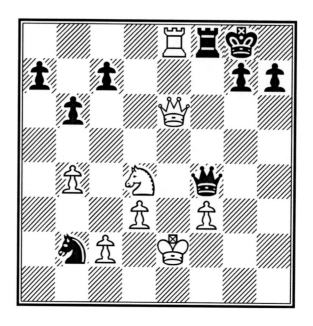

Conversely, other chess players like to play very conservatively, taking no risks, defending solidly, and waiting for one moment of weakness in the opposition. A good example of this was Karpov, a great rival of Kasparov, whose style of play was often criticised for being too unadventurous. As he said himself,

> 'Sometimes I am criticized for being dry, rational, calculating. Yes I am pragmatic....I try to play 'correct' chess and never take risks'.

This is the very same attitude that Italian club teams, and the national team, have had for many years. Their philosophy is to maintain a watertight defence so that the opposition cannot score, and then try to score one goal on the counter-attack. Many consider this a boring and negative way of playing football and chess. However, in his book *Defence in Chess* Andrew Soltis defends this method of playing:

> 'Stonewalling has a bad reputation because it is essentially negative and passive. The emphasis is on holding the line, not conceding anything. But the defender has the psychological edge of having established the ground rules for play... the onus is on the aggressor to make something of the position'.

Karpov actually got more satisfaction from playing this style of chess than any other:

> 'If the opponent offers keen play I don't object; but in such cases I get less satisfaction, even if I win, than from a game conducted according to all the rules of strategy with its ruthless logic.'

This ruthless logic is something that Italian football also seems to have a taste for, and many top Italian teams are never more pleased with themselves than when they have won 1-0. Indeed, it should be remembered that this style persists not only because of a desperate desire to win at all costs, but because players and supporters enjoy it. As the famous Italian coach Ariggo Sacchi explains, 'I remember once a match with Juventus and Milan; after 15 minutes Juventus hit the goal and basically the match ended then. And for the audience it was just fine.'

It seems Karpov's style was as much an extension of his personality as a belief about the best way of winning. Indeed both games have an extraordinary ability to allow individual personality as much as character to be expressed through them, and this constitutes one of the main reasons why so many people love chess and football. 'I am convinced, the way one plays chess always reflects the player's personality. If something defines his character, then it will also define his way of playing' declares Kramnik. He adds, 'For me art and chess are closely related, both are forms in which the self finds beauty and expression.' One need only watch the World Cup to see that the same is true in football. Different nations have very distinctive types of football that they have played for many generations.

EVOLUTION OF THE GAMES

The evolution of the games from the point of view of theory and tactics has been very similar. During the nineteenth century, chess was played in a wildly attacking manner with little concern for defence. Games were open and exciting. However, just before the turn of the century GM Steinitz offered the world a new theory about the way chess should be played. He emphasised a solid defence and careful positional play, believing that powerful attacks were only possible because of defensive mistakes. He was successful in demonstrating the veracity of these theories in many of his games, and gradually other Grandmasters began to become more defensively minded and aware of positioning. Since the tempo of the games slowed down as a result, an emphasis was placed on what Steinitz called 'the accumulation of small advantages'. Instead of dramatic attacking play with exciting sacrifices, he would slowly grind the opponent down over the course of the game.

The positional rules on which Steinitz placed such an emphasis were taken up by Grandmasters as the route towards finding the most 'correct' way to play. It became a case of eliminating all mistakes and finding the 'ultimate' way to play chess so that you could not be beaten. The generation of champions after Steinitz certainly thought they had managed to find this 'truth' in chess. They believed that all the rules for playing correct chess had been learnt and that, as a result, most games would end up a stalemate. Indeed Capablanca said at the time that it was 'difficult to win a game, even against a weaker player'. The overall feeling at the time was that chess had reached the end of the road. It was 'dead'. Its mystery had been uncovered.

Of course, chess was not going to stagnate that easily. Little did the chess players of the time realise that they had only really scratched the surface of the game in their play. Their method of playing was, according to John Watson, 'unimaginative and limited in several respects' and 'blind to the flexibility of modern play'. Such limitations were made apparent by a new style of play which has developed over the course of the twentieth century. The modern 'dynamic' school of chess approaches the game from a less static point of view and sees the limitations of sticking to absolute rules. The new school of thought maintains that each position should be judged on its own merit and not according to what positional dogma would suggest. For GM Reti, the dynamic chess player tries 'not to treat every position according to one general law, but according to the principle inherent in that position'. GM Mihai Suba goes on to explain that 'seemingly poor, restricted positions may be good ones' whilst a 'fine, unrestricted position which is seemingly better, may sometimes actually be worse'.

The evolution of football tactics has followed a strikingly similar path to that of chess. In the early decades the most commonly used formation was the ultra attacking 2-3-5. As with nineteenth-century chess, it seemed logical that, since the point was to score goals, you needed as many attackers as possible. Gradually, however, teams started to adopt a more defensive strategy. Like Steinitz, coaches realised that most goals were being scored because of defensive errors rather than attacking brilliance. If a team could cut out these errors and defend 'correctly' then they would be half way towards winning. The most extreme adherence to this philosophy could be found amongst the Italians who adopted the 'catenaccio' (door-bolt) system. Like Steinitz, the Italians placed a heavy emphasis on correct positioning and attempted, as far as possible, to eliminate risk from their game. The effect was that the games were played at a slower tempo and the amount of goals scored dramatically decreased. Now it was the small details that made all the difference. Teams learnt to defend more tightly and attacking players were given less and less options. Thus, reckless attacking play from the opposition would be easily stifled.

Such is the level of defensive solidarity amongst modern teams that many people have the same view of football that Capablanca had of chess in the 1930s: that teams have learnt tactical procedures to cancel each other out. Like chess at the time, weaker teams can force a draw against stronger teams because they know how to organise themselves to play 'correctly'. This has led to comments like those of Brazilian coach Phil Scholari, who has stated that 'the beautiful game is dead'.

However, whilst it is possible to hold such a pessimistic view, it should also be remembered that there are other philosophies in the modern age of football that have successfully rebelled against this idea. For instance, the attack-minded Ajax philosophy that has been in place since the 1970s has enabled various teams that have followed to win the European Cup. In fact, the philosophy is very similar to the modern 'dynamic' school of chess. Instead of regurgitating standard ideas about the 'correct' way to play, Ajax try to instil in their players an intelligence which will enable them to consider each situation on its own terms and come up with a suitable solution. As the coach of the 1995 Champions League winning side Louis Van Gaal says, 'we teach players to be creative in their thinking, and that each situation on the field is different. It is all about choosing the right answer for each situation.' This echoes GM Reti's description of the modern school of chess. Van Gaal's assertion that 'it is all about somebody being positive, creative, being able to find an opening that others do not see' can be equated to the attributes of Garry Kasparov's dynamic style of chess.

Perhaps more football managers could reflect on the way modern Grandmasters have reinvigorated chess. Certainly, Arsene Wenger seems to consider it his mission to play a 'dynamic' style of football which can overcome what many would call defensive negativity: 'It is important for the game that the teams and the coaches take the initiative. I know we live in a world where we have only winners and losers, but once a sport encourages teams who refuse to take the initiative, the sport is in danger.'

When Wenger joined Arsenal he stated his desire to play 'real, modern football' based on his long held beliefs that football should be played with 'speed and dynamism'. It turned out his idea of 'modern' football was very similar to the concept of 'modern' chess. Like Kasparov, Wenger's style of football involved taking calculated risks. Furthermore, in the same way that much of the 'dynamism' of modern chess comes from Grandmasters thinking more deeply about combinations, Arsene Wenger introduced a style of football which placed a far higher emphasis on combinations than English football had every seen before. The result was a record breaking run of 49 games unbeaten in the Premiership and the admiration of millions for playing 'beautiful' football.

THE BEAUTIFUL GAMES

'The reason why football is loved so much is because it has no definite truth'. Michel Platini.

'Sometimes I think I have understood a position, but after a couple of years I realize that I have understood nothing. That is what is so mysterious and fascinating about chess.' GM Kramnik

What is the soul of chess? Is it an art or a science? What about football? What exactly makes it 'the beautiful game'? These questions cannot be answered with any certainty. As with a great melody we can do all the analysis we want, but there will always remain an abstract mystery at the heart of it that we cannot uncover. This, perhaps, contributes to the endless fascination people have with both games. As the great chess player Tarrasch stated so simply, 'chess, like music and love, has the power to make men happy'. The same can undoubtedly be said for football, given its world-wide popularity.

For many chess players, trying to find the meaning of chess seems to be almost as challenging as finding the meaning of life itself. As GM Bronstein said rather mysteriously 'the essence of chess is thinking about what chess is'. For GM Fine, 'It is because combinations are possible that Chess is more than a lifeless mathematical exercise. They are the poetry of the game; they are to Chess what melody is to music. They represent the triumph of mind over matter'. Many would agree that it is the exciting, dynamic elements of the games that make them 'beautiful'. However, there is a concurrent school of thought which appreciates the more subtle side, in much the same way that you can admire both the complexity and simplicity of nature:

'I continue to be excited in chess by the amazing world of ideas and beauty. For me chess aesthetics signify, most of all, the correctness of an idea, its truth, revealed in clear logic of thought. Beauty manifests itself not only in combinative play and spectacular sacrifices, but also in a seemingly simple position, when the richness of its content is suddenly discovered'. GM Smyslov.

The great Dutch footballer, Johan Cruyff, who enjoys philosophising about football, takes a similar line: 'simple football is the most beautiful.' His team-mate Ruud Krol expands on this: 'It is the same with artists. The best work is not difficult, it is very simple.'

In the world of modern football where winning seems to be paramount above all else, it is easy for teams to dismiss the need to play attractive, honest football. Many people believe, as the Brazilian coach Phil Scholari has stated, that 'the beautiful game is dead'. However, it should not be ignored that tremendous pressure can be brought to bear upon teams that don't satisfy the public appetite for 'beautiful' football played in a good spirit. Chelsea, under Mourinho, made themselves very unpopular with fans and journalists across England because their football was not seen as entertaining enough and their methods unsporting. For journalist James Lawton, it was not Chelsea's riches which he found ugly, but the type of football developed by Jose Mourinho whose 'ruthlessness and efficiency' (characteristics instilled into his team) could, 'guarantee trophies but not lasting glory'. And whilst Mourinho might answer that trophies are tangible whereas 'glory' is just a subjectively issued noun, other coaches, like Arsene Wenger and Johan Cruyff, believe a team can only achieve true greatness through playing attractive football. Cruyff believes that 'football should always be played beautifully. You should play in an attacking way, it must be a spectacle.' A similar debate exists in the chess world. The great Lasker challenged Tarrasch's view of chess, saying 'my opponent believes in beauty. I believe in strength. I believe that by being strong a move is beautiful too'.

But whilst it may be impossible to find a definite truth in either game, perhaps they can be compared with other arts to find out what abstract qualities lie within the games that suggest to us their importance as more than just games. In music, composers start off with endless rhythmic, harmonic and melodic possibilities of combining notes. Out of this chaos they are able to craft coherent and meaningful melodies and harmonies. A parallel can be found in football and chess - with every connection we build and with every line we create we are making order out of chaos. We start with a blank canvas and on to it we throw patterns, shapes, ideas. We are in a process of creation. The greater the quality of the chess or football, the greater is this sense that they are arts. In a single brilliant move by Mikhail Tal can be found intuition, logic, clarity, courage, aggression and devastation - a beautiful combination of the delicate and the ferocious. So too can we find these things in a great pass by Ronaldinho. Great moves contain an intellectual and emotional depth which invest them with artistic qualities. Herein, perhaps, is where the art and beauty of football and chess lie.

THE FUTURE

Football has progressed tremendously over the last 30 years. The quality and complexity of teams has never been higher. However, many fans see the new emphasis on tactics as a threat to their enjoyment of the game. Unfortunately for them, football was always destined to evolve in this way because it is in its very nature a highly tactical game. Games in the past were more open and afforded players more time and space to express themselves individually because understanding of football was not as highly developed as it is now. This preoccupation with tactics has arisen not because winning is more important and teams are afraid of losing, but because more coaches understand the basic concept that collective harmony is more powerful than individual excellence.

In the light of these changes, I believe that playing chess can help fans and players alike to develop their understanding of football. The beneficial influence of chess on the human intellect and character are continually demonstrated by studies. Garry Kasparov sums this up: 'Results show that just one year of chess tuition will improve a student's learning abilities, concentration, application, sense of logic, self-discipline, respect, behavior and the ability to take responsibility for his/her own actions'. Whilst it may take a scientific study to convince people that playing chess can improve a person's respect and behaviour, it is far more easy to accept that chess improves a person's spatial awareness. A person who is learning chess can only improve by developing certain faculties such as spatial awareness, concentration and strategic evaluation. Given that these are the very faculties that one uses when playing football, it makes sense that playing chess should benefit anybody who plays football.

It is interesting that players discussing the methods of the chess-playing coaches Rafael Benitez and Karel Bruckner say very similar things about them. The Czech Republic goalkeeper Petr Czech places great value on the tactical preparations Bruckner makes before games: 'Most of the time, everything he says before the game usually happens during the game. Or there is some period when you can really feel he understands what's happening on the pitch and it's a huge help. Everything he wants to do on the pitch we trust is the right way to play'. Czech continues, 'he can read the system of our opponents very well tactically, and is very well prepared for each opponent. Sometimes this makes the main difference in games.' The Liverpool defender Jamie Carragher describes similar qualities in Benitez: 'We work a lot on tactics as a team, how the team is going to play and the weaknesses of our opponents. We probably do more tactical work now than I have done with any manager at any level in my career. That's how he likes to do things. When he has the time to prepare the team properly you can see that it's reflected in the performances.'

On the other hand, it should be equally rewarding for chess players to develop an interest in football. The deep satisfaction that chess players experience through the use of their pieces harmoniously and destructively is an experience confined to an individual. Many would find it more satisfying to experience such harmony collectively, as part of a group of people. 'Fancy what a game at chess would be if all the chessmen had passions and intellects' comments the narrator in George Eliot's *Felix Holt*. Football offers this possibility.

BIBLIOGRAPHY

Crouch, Colin. *How to Defend in Chess.* London: Everyman Chess, 2000.

Edgar, Bill. 'Chelsea Killjoys rile Wenger' *The Times* 24/6/05

Glanville, Brian. 'Ajax Supreme' *Champions League Guide*, Issue 1. 84.

Kasparov, Garry. *My Great Predecessors: part II.* London: Everyman chess, 2003.

Kormelink, Henry. *The Coaching Philosophies of Louis Van Gaal and the Ajax Coaches* Spring City: Reedswain, 1995.

Lasker, Emmanuel. *Lasker's Manuel of Chess* Mineloa: Dover 1960.

Loret, Paco. *Rafa Benitez: The Authorised Biography* Dewi Lewis Media Ltd, 2005.

Michels, Renus. *Teambuilding: the Road to Success* Spring City: Reedswain, 2001.

Nimzowitsch, Aron. *My system.* London: Everyman Chess, 2000.

Palmer, Myles. *The professor: Arsene Wenger at Arsenal.* Virgin books, 2005.

Short, Nigel. *Chess Basics.* Sterling Publishing, 1994.

Silman, Jeremy. *The Complete Book of Chess strategy.* Los Angeles: Siles Press, 1998.

Soltis, Andrew. *The Art of Defence in Chess* Random House, 2003.

Trappatoni, Giovanni. *Coaching High Performance Soccer* Spring City: Reedswain, 2000.

Watson, John. *Secrets of Modern Chess Strategy* London: Gambit, 1999.

Winner, David. *Brilliant Orange: The Neurotic Genius of Dutch Football.* London: Bloomsbury, 2001.

Winter, Henry. 'Cantona still backs flair to beat the system'. *Daily Telegraph* 08/02/06.

Zauli, Alessandro. *Soccer: Modern Tactics* Spring City: Reedswain, 2002.

'How relaxed Chelsea took complete control'. *Guardian Unlimited* 15/10/2005.

Lightning Source UK Ltd.
Milton Keynes UK
08 December 2009

147208UK00002B/87/P